CW01024151

'Beautifully written and accessible, *Covenant* turns political theory into practical policy – applying the old conservative truths to the challenges of the 21st century. In future Conservatives will point to this book and say, as Margaret Thatcher did, "this is what we believe!"'

Tim Stanley, Daily Telegraph columnist

'In this erudite and important book, Danny Kruger shows that the answers to our very modern problems lie not in the ideological dysfunctions of liberalism, but in the norms, customs and insights we once understood but tragically have instead rejected and forgotten'

Nick Timothy, former Chief of Staff to Theresa May

'In an age when most self-identified "conservatives" are little more than disaster capitalists with a side order of culture war, Danny Kruger stands out. This book shows why: Kruger possesses not only a thorough grasp of the conservative tradition, but also an appropriate realism about present-day challenges and the need not just to conserve but also to rebuild'

Mary Harrington, author of Feminism Against Progress

'Danny Kruger's *Covenant* is a gem of a book, offering a new vision for British conservatism that would replace the decaying "social contract" with a much stronger, covenantal interpretation of our obligations to family, community, and nation. Packed with common-sense policy proposals, it is also a personal declaration of faith in a restored Britain that is almost within reach'

Yoram Hazony, author of Conservatism: A Rediscovery

'Danny Kruger has written a brilliant and blistering blueprint for a politics of national renewal. Fizzing with philosophical and historical insight and brimming with common sense, he offers a manifesto for realising the common good and healing our fractured political landscape. Kruger's charter for a new conservatism represents the most promising organising idea for public policy to emerge for many years'

James Orr, Chair, Edmund Burke Foundation UK

'What a rare pleasure to read a book by a politician that avoids the usual dead, bureaucratic, policy prose and asks fundamental questions about how to live and how to organise a society that transcends the liberal individualism-cum-utilitarianism of mainstream politics. A post-liberal, Scrutonian manifesto for conservatives'

David Goodhart, author of The Road to Somewhere

'*Covenant* is required reading for anyone concerned about the current state of politics and society. A powerful and urgent critique of the ruling liberalism, this passionate manifesto for a new kind of conservatism will engage readers on every part of the political spectrum. If you are dissatisfied with the ideas that govern us, Danny Kruger has something of vital interest to say to you'

John Gray, political philosopher

COVENANT

The New Politics of Home,
Neighbourhood and Nation

Danny Kruger

FORUM

First published in Great Britain by Forum, an imprint of Swift Press 2023

1 3 5 7 9 8 6 4 2

Copyright © Danny Kruger 2023

The right of Danny Kruger to be identified as the Author of this Work has been asserted in accordance with the Copyright, Designs and Patents Act 1988.

Printed and bound in Great Britain by CPI Group (UK) Ltd, Croydon, CRO 4YY

A CIP catalogue record for this book is available from the British Library

ISBN: 9781800752115
eISBN: 9781800752122

CONTENTS

Foreword

THE NEW CONSERVATISM

There is nothing new in conservatism, though from time to time a new generation finds a fresh way to say the old things, perhaps with some discomfort for the generation that went before. Today, the late twentieth-century battle cry against global communism and domestic socialism – and its early twenty-first-century echo, exhorting the further march of liberalism at home and abroad – is being challenged by a different analysis and a different plan. We are witnessing a powerful popular and intellectual resurgence within conservatism, looking back to the fundamentals of the creed and forward to a meaningful engagement with the tech-driven challenges of the new century.

Today's 'New Conservatives' are less concerned with maximising opportunities for individual freedom than with shoring up the conditions that make freedom possible. These conditions are the institutions of social life: families, communities, nations, and the virtues that sustain them. Put most simply, we need to strengthen the economic, social and cultural forces that make good people.

This argument represents a major challenge to the political orthodoxies of recent times. Yet the solutions to our difficulties lie deeper in our history, and particularly in the history told by conservatives: the steady development and defence over centuries of the institutions that make up the common life of the United Kingdom. And the eternal paradox of conservatism is that this deference to the past fits us for the future: a respect for institutions – and for the foundational institutions of family, community and nation most of all – is the best possible attitude with which to approach modernity. With this attitude, we can make modernity safe and fruitful, as well as respectful of the virtues and the institutions that we need.

Conservatism is the proper basis for prosperity in the age of tech. This is because conservatism entails change, sometimes radical change, at least on the surface. The particular forms by which we organise our common life – our social, economic and political practices – can and must adapt as our material capabilities develop and as new dangers emerge: this book argues for some profound changes in light of the threats and opportunities of the times. But the conservative remembers that the purpose of these practices is simply to sustain the community of the people, that the reason for change is to stay the same.

This book is largely a compendium of ideas I have picked up from writers in this old-new, radical-reactionary tradition. I try to acknowledge the leading exponents of particular points in the endnotes. But more generally, I here state my gratitude to the philosopher-theologians Alasdair MacIntyre, John Gray and John Milbank; to the political theorists and policy thinkers Phillip Blond, Hilary Cottam, Sir Paul Collier, David Goodhart, Matthew Goodwin, Maurice Glasman, Mary Harrington, Polly Mackenzie, Adrian Pabst, Louise Perry, Nina Power, Nick Timothy and David Skelton; to my old friends – the first proper conservatives I met in the Conservative Party – the commentators Tim Montgomerie and Peter Franklin; and of course, with profound reverence, to the late Sir Roger Scruton. I am also inspired by a number of great American writers on similar themes, from the prophets Philip Rieff, Robert Putnam and Charles Murray to today's 'post-liberals' Yoram Hazony, Patrick Deneen, Sohrab Ahmari, Carl Trueman and Oren Cass.

Not all these writers, it should be noted, are on the political Right, and not all will agree with everything that follows. I cite them, whether they like it or not, because I detect that across the old party divide, which we still use to demarcate our allegiances, a bigger loyalty is growing. This loyalty is to what I call the 'covenant' on which Western politics is founded. The covenant is threatened in this generation by a malignant growth within liberalism, which has already effectively killed that creed and is coming for the rest of us. Conservatives, communitarians, refugee liberals (those who actually believe in liberty), even socialists and anarchists, all have a common cause: to defend the covenant and restore the proper basis of freedom.

For their inspiration and guidance as I wrote this book I am particularly grateful to my friends at the New Social Covenant Unit, including the parliamentary colleagues we work with; my co-chair Miriam Cates MP; Sam Armstrong; and most of all Imogen Sinclair, with whom I have happily bounced the ideas that appear in this book back and forth for years. My thanks also to David Johnston MP who, though he disagrees with me on much, kindly read the book closely and made suggestions for improvement, some of which I have taken.

The book is dedicated, with love, to my wife Emma, who stands for everything I believe in.

Introduction

ON MORGAN'S HILL

If a 'place' is ground made meaningful by human beings, the central district of Wiltshire must be the oldest place in England. Here our Neolithic forbears built the monuments of their now-silent civilisation: the long and the round barrows; the huge mounds like Silbury Hill (the largest man-made structure of Western prehistory); and the standing stones and circles, like Stonehenge and the older and bigger Avebury, and largest of all but now almost vanished, the great henge at Marden.

Why here, on these downs? Perhaps a reason is that here rise the three rivers that between them water most of southern England. A drop of rain falling on Morgan's Hill, north of Devizes, can flow west with the Bristol Avon to the Atlantic Ocean, south with the Hampshire Avon to the English Channel, or east with the Kennet to the Thames and the North Sea. Maybe the ancient people knew this, and they felt that this was special ground: the source-place.

We don't know how Neolithic civilisation ended, although there are signs of war across Europe around the time that the monuments became disused. Yet the sacred streams never suffered, flowing full and clear through the ages – until now. Today, the Avons and the Kennet, like almost all the rivers of England, are low in volume because we extract so much water for our homes and businesses; they are full of artificial nutrients that choke them with weeds, and they are regularly flooded with raw sewage.

As a metaphor for the way we are living, it serves. We are polluting the sources of life. Our treatment of our habitat reflects the self-destructive bent our society is on, which starts with nature and will end with us. For society, too, is depleted, contaminated, and at risk. And so our own great monuments, our modern henges and standing stones – our towers and temples, our intelligent machines, our magical devices for cosmic communication, erected with such effort and ingenuity to awe and astonish – face the fate of the Neolithic ones: to be ruins, grassy hummocks, broken masonry on the bare hills, and only bones in holes to speak of who we were.

The conservative is disposed to be gloomy. History, as Tolkein said, is a 'long defeat', a steady attrition of value and spirit under the shadow of the possibility of absolute disaster. And today more than ever, we in the West have reasons to be fearful. Since the turn of the millennium, we have been in a state of chronic war – persistent, multi-domain, hot and cold by turns, and apparently unwinnable – against Islamist groups and states in North Africa, the Middle East and central Asia, and sometimes on our own soil.

In 2008, the global financial system came close to collapse and was only kept together by a huge injection of newly minted money, which disproportionately flowed into the pockets of the already wealthy and held back the prosperity of the public for a decade. In 2020–21, the coronavirus pandemic caused governments – in all good faith, with public support, and perhaps unavoidably – to inflict a social and economic catastrophe on their populations. And in 2022, war erupted once more in Europe, launched by a tyrant who plausibly threatens nuclear war. Meanwhile, we have entered a new polarity, with a weakening West facing a strengthening China, whose rulers are at least as pitiless and aggrandising as Russia's.

The new millennium has not started well, and it could be about to get worse. Traditional threats like military dictatorships, terrorism and the rivalry of superpowers are now augmented by more complex enemies. Humanity is threatened by the collapse of systems.

The interlinked technologies of the world, the supply chains, data webs and energy grids that sustain modern life, are uniquely vulnerable to attack or accident. The global

economy is perched precariously on a growing and increasingly unstable mountain of debt because the problems that
caused the 2008 crisis have not been addressed but exacerbated in the years since: the world is leveraged against faith,
so far out beyond the pivot that the slightest evaporation of
confidence could cause a crash.

Meanwhile, the health of humanity is imperilled by the
growing ineffectiveness of antibiotics and the ease of conta-
gion: imagine a lethal pandemic that, like the Spanish Flu
of 1918, attacks the young and healthy and mutates faster
than our vaccines. War is assuming hideous modern forms,
involving robots, cyber attacks and bioweapons that could
cripple whole countries, or destroy races, at the touch of a
button or the crack of a vial.

The age of tech offers an enticing set of solutions to the
threats that beset us. We are offered free, limitless, ecologi-
cally harmless energy, sources of robot labour that will make
'work' in the traditional sense redundant, and medical mir-
acles that will conquer all illness and maybe even vanquish
death itself. Yet we are speeding into the future without the
vaguest sense of what these possibilities imply for the things
that matter: our sense of ourselves, our relationships with
one another, and our place in nature.

In our addiction to progress we are unable to distinguish
between mere technological innovation and actual improvements in the condition of mankind. Artificial intelligence
is learning fast. The singularity – the moment when tech

becomes fully autonomous and unstoppable – is coming. We have little idea as a civilisation how to manage this revolution.

It is no surprise that the great Earth system itself is in danger, with a range of catastrophic ecological tipping points now in view, such as a 'blue ocean' event in the Arctic, the melting of the permafrost, or runaway fires in the Amazon. The threats of such catastrophes may be exaggerated; the eschatology of climate alarmism is itself deeply harmful and inhuman; and surely many of the remedies proposed would bring catastrophes of their own. But even without an apocalyptic tipping point, the risk is real that large parts of Africa, India and China will become deserts, while coastal regions, the centres of the economy and population in many countries, will disappear under the sea.

Already, the pressure on land and water is intense. In the decades to come, it is likely that refugees will destabilise their own and neighbouring countries, stoking civil conflict, terrorism and war – and mass migration, on a scale that will dwarf the movements of people that have already transformed the societies (and the politics) of Europe in this century. Tens of millions of desperate migrants will head north and west from Africa, the Middle East and Asia towards our safe and temperate continent, and especially towards the rich and rainy archipelago off its western edge.

*

How ready are we in the United Kingdom, not just for mass migration but for the other system threats? How strong is society here at home?

These islands, providentially situated in a cool corner of the globe, surrounded by sea and then by friendly, democratic nations, with a powerful economy and a uniquely creative spirit of innovation, with strong defences, a tradition of law and a long history of civil peace, with historic links to all corners of the globe, which gave the world its principal language and much of its culture – surely these islands are well placed, physically and culturally, to face the challenges of the times. Yet these natural advantages are belied by some serious weaknesses.

On the face of it, our economic system seems robust. We have a pro-business environment, with some exuberantly successful firms, sectors and places. But these mask what is shown in the national statistics – the far less prosperous reality everywhere else. Years of artificially low interest rates and an artificially strong pound have given us a sense of being richer than we really are; rising rates and a weakening pound will adjust our impressions painfully. Meanwhile, tax, public spending and public and private debt are at their highest levels since World War II. In general, our productivity is woeful and we have a long tail of low-value businesses, particularly outside the South East and the big cities.

The UK is the most spatially unequal country in the developed world. Our economy is chronically unbalanced, but not just between north and south, or the productive and the rest. The worst unbalance is in the least enterprising sector of all, but the one that matters most to most people. The extreme inflation of house prices and housing costs, pumped up by the low interest rates and money-printing of the last twenty years, sustains a rentier class of landlords and property owners in permanent supremacy over the asset-poor majority. Even the rentiers are, perversely, slaves to debt, indentured to their mortgages, which rising rates will make cruelly heavy.

The effect of all this is extreme stress on the understanding that, by making inequality tolerable, holds society together: the knowledge that a brighter day is coming, that everyone has a decent chance of a good life, and that each generation will be better off than the one before it.

The economic reality is reflected in the state of society. The upshot, at its most pitiable, are the 'deaths of despair' described by Angus Deaton: the phenomenon of deaths from drugs and alcohol, suicide and chronic ill-health induced by diet and lifestyle.[1] But more generally, we have not deaths but lives of despair. We have epidemics of mental ill-health, domestic abuse and loneliness. We are bored and anxious. We distract and medicate ourselves with a cocktail of passive entertainment, legal and illegal drugs, alcohol and bad food.

As a nation, we are both obese and undernourished, a neat reflection of a society rich in some respects and not in others. The government spends over £150 billion per year – a sixth of national expenditure, 1.5 times the education budget and three times more than we spend on defence – on 'social protection', namely support for people who struggle.[2] And it is not enough: even with all this welfare, a quarter of the population lives in households with an income that is inadequate for an acceptable standard of living.[3]

If our economy and society – the fundamental systems on which we each depend – are in some trouble, what of the state? The United Kingdom has much to be proud of in the millions of front-line public servants who maintain the systems that look after us, from the army to the health service. And yet, the state of the state itself – our system of government and the leadership of public bodies – suggests both a profound weakness and a profound threat. Like much of the population itself, public services are simultaneously over-fed and undernourished: they consume ever more public money, and yet there is never enough money for the front line. The National Health Service, in particular, is over-centralised and over-bureaucratic, with costs controlled through rationing and pseudo-market mechanisms, and consequently – though no one intends this and everyone tries to prevent it – it is frequently uncaring in its dealings with both citizens and its own staff.

The endemic tendency of the public sector to centralisation and top-down control reflects the last great threat in my litany of dangers. This is the creation, in response to a crisis – like a new pandemic, or a war, or a melting icecap – of an apparatus of state control that will complete the ruin.

Covid-19 exposed a state unready for disaster, lacking in the most essential elements of resilience: capacity in the health service for a population-wide illness, domestic supply chains in place to cope with a sudden stop to global trade, and systems ready to go for the support of the vulnerable. The state cranked into gear during 2020 to address these requirements. But at the same time, it found for itself a far easier task than organising the needs of the people: creating rules for them to follow. The government – with the support of MPs including, I am ashamed to say, myself – passed laws that suspended the basic civil liberties of the country and gave ministers sweeping powers to curtail them further as required. These laws have now been repealed, but the precedent is established. And more generally, we have grown used to the principle that the answer to a threat is government enforcing universal solutions.

The response to Covid-19 was a ramshackle harbinger of the far more professional apparatus of state control we can expect in future. This time it was universal testing, universal lockdown, universal vaccination; what universal system will be imposed next time? The apparatus will be enabled by technology, by the extraordinary new possibilities of digital and biomedical surveillance, artificial intelligence and autonomous robotics, and authorised by politicians anxiously agreeing with the media that 'something must be done' to mitigate this threat or address that injustice. The politicians will credulously accept the assurances of the peddlers of tech that the problem will be fixed quickly, cheaply and without the public minding. And they may be right about the public, for the apparatus will be propelled by an understandable fear in the general population at the threats I have outlined: by our desire for spells and amulets to ward off danger and by our never-to-be-underestimated willingness to trade our freedom for our safety.

It is possible to be paranoid about the intentions of government and its agents in the private sector who enable and profit from the expansion of state power. But the threat is very real. China stands before us as evidence of the dystopic possibility of what Paul Kingsnorth, following Kevin Kelly, calls 'the technium': the aggregated machinery of the digital age which forms a single omnipotent intelligence.[4] The apparatus is most fully developed in China, with a complete system of tech-enabled state surveillance, complete with 'social credits' that reward and punish citizens for their compliance with the rules. China gave us the defining moment of Covid-19: the drone flying between the tower blocks of locked-down Shanghai, intoning from its speaker the recorded message 'Suppress your soul's desire for freedom. Do not open your window to sing.' Welcome to the future.

*

The way to clean a river is to act wide and deep, patiently and holistically, with a combination of 'grey and green' interventions: concrete infrastructure to manage the effects of large-scale human activity, and nature-based solutions to conserve and clean the water and soil. Given that we build houses whose design prodigiously wastes water, we do need more 'grey' work: more pipes and sewage treatment works. But 'grey' can never be sufficient: we will never pour enough concrete to meet current and projected demand. We need to reduce demand on the infrastructure and we need better solutions than concrete. 'Green' interventions – catchment-wide mitigation, better farming practices, better planning and housebuilding design, reed beds that filter dirty water naturally – are the long-term, sustainable answers to pollution, water loss and soil erosion.[*]

We also need a 'grey and green' strategy for the system risks we face. Much must be done by government to build and maintain the structures and services of our national life and adapt them to today's opportunities and threats. But this 'grey' work is not enough. It can never be enough, and if we focus only on statutory structures and services – on what government can do, whether directly or by regulation – we will see demand build and build, like a drain backing up with dirty water.

---

[*] This combined strategy is the basis of the government's 'Plan for Water' (updated April 2023).

More important than the 'grey' work of the state is the 'green' work done by each of us towards each other. The principal agency in society is society itself, from the businesses we work in and buy from; to the social institutions that we belong to, serve and are served by; to our families and all the people that we call 'we', whether neighbours or some other community of interest. These are the nature-based solutions to the harm we are doing to our habitat. Here is the system we need to clean up the mess we are making.

This book does not attempt to grapple directly with the whole bewilderment of threats that our country faces. Rather, I try to describe a theory about why we in the United Kingdom, and across the West more generally, are where we are, what we are doing wrong, and how, in principle, to put things right.

Edmund Burke wrote in a letter to a friend that 'the sources of the commonwealth are in the households'.* I suggest that the sources of our prosperity and our common life lie in the deep aquifer of Western ideas about personhood and social relations, centred on the home and household. In neglecting, indeed polluting, this source, we are harming the thing that gives society its life. And in restoring the health of this source we can revive our society, defend ourselves against system threats, and move

---

* 'To corrupt family relations is to poison fountains; for the sources of the commonwealth are in the households; and errors there are irretrievable.' Edmund Burke, letter to Edmund Sexton Perry, 16 June 1778.

forward to a safer and better future. But first, we must understand our mistake.

The governing paradigm of modern Western politics is the 'social contract'. Simply put, this is the imaginary deal by which we each surrender our use of physical force to a strong central state – the 'common power, to keep men in awe', as Thomas Hobbes put it in 1651 – in exchange for its protection of our life, liberty and property. In Britain in the years following Hobbes, thanks particularly to John Locke, this deal acquired a particularly liberal flavour: the 'common power' came to be exercised by Parliament and was itself limited by the law that applied to everyone equally, even the state. We obey the law, and pay our taxes, and we are then free to do, and importantly to believe and to speak, as we please.

The model of government that between them Hobbes and Locke gave us – a state with a monopoly of force, accountable to Parliament, limited by law and protective of the freedoms of speech and belief – is a good one, indeed the best one possible; it can be said to have driven the great explosion of commercial, scientific and intellectual innovation that made Britain great in the eighteenth and nineteenth centuries. And yet the social contract had a founding flaw: the idea of this model as the free creation of each of us.

Hobbes and Locke found the sources of English liberty not in the customs of the country, in the practices of

accommodation and settlement passed down the generations, but in 'reason', the intelligence which Locke said
'teaches all mankind, who will but consult it'. It is reason,
thought Locke, that induces us each to enter 'mutually...
the body politic'. And so the very basis of society, according
to this theory, is imaginary, a decision made in the mind
of humankind; society itself is self-made, with at its heart
the solitary, self-determining, 'free' individual who voluntarily consented to (and by this consent created) the social
arrangement he or she lives under.[5]

The imagined origin of a society determines its path.
It has taken centuries, but in modern times we have come
to fulfil the implicit end or purpose that Locke aimed us
at. Under the social contract, government is the creation
of the sovereign individual. Like all creatures, it is constructed to honour its creator. Government's job is the facilitation of personal independence, and the mitigation of its
consequences. The essential mission of organised society
thus becomes to dissolve the relationships between people,
to obviate the necessity of cooperation, and to make each
person as far as possible a solitary, autonomous, independent
being.

This is the doctrine of social justice in its fulfilled understanding: the abstraction of people from the contexts they
inhabit; a society where people are liberated from the relationships that limit and diminish them, where 'it doesn't
matter where you come from'. Two salient implementations

of this doctrine were initiated by Tony Blair's government in the first years of this century: the free movement of people to the UK from across the whole continent of Europe, and the huge expansion of university education. Free movement has been curtailed by Brexit (albeit we now import even more people from further abroad than Europe). But the rush to the universities continues apace.

This trend is particularly significant in terms of the intellectual culture of the country. Every year, we induce nearly half the cohort of school leavers to leave their home towns to study in a distant city. Here they are tutored by academics and socialised by other students steeped in the philosophy of liberation, and thus cleansed of whatever provincial mores they arrived at university with. They study for degrees that give them no prospect of a well-paid job, but the immediate reality of a large debt. These students then stay in their university city, or perhaps drift to London or Manchester. And so they swell the ranks of the precariat: overqualified, underpaid and paying exorbitant rents for homes they can never hope to own.[6]

Modern liberation theory is even more abstract, and abstracting, than former versions. Marxism has become cultural, and the dehumanising, deracinating effects Marx ascribed to the processes of capitalism ('all that is solid melts into air, and all that is holy is profaned') are now joyfully promoted by his heirs. The conditions of justice are no longer material, the blunt realities of capital and labour, but ethereal, a swirl of intersectional and identitarian factors that, resolving themselves into a new hierarchy of oppression and victimhood, serve only to cancel the attachments and affections the student has, or had, or should have, for his or her home. And where the cancellation is not complete, when some residue of natural loyalty is rashly expressed, power is summoned, in the form of a censorious new religiosity at least as forbidding and humourless as the sort Marx knew in Victorian England.

It is a simple paradox that a doctrine of unreality results in some very real mechanisms to enforce the fantasy, and that the facilitation of individual independence leads quickly and easily to oppression. The dissolution of relationships necessitates a culture of insistent conformity and a vast alternative apparatus of social support. For the facilitation of independence is a job not for a small state but for a big one. And naturally, the apparatus is not always kindly in its operations. Dissolved relationships have ugly effects, and social distress manifests itself anti-socially. The apparatus then leans not towards Locke, with his stress on personal freedom, but back towards Hobbes, and his 'common power': compulsion, enforcement and – dread word to people dependent on benefits – 'sanction'.

Facilitation of independence, mitigation of the social and personal disarray that follows, and sanctions when patience snaps: these are the functions of a state built on the social contract. The effect is a system that is at once over-generous and over-harsh, too soft and too hard all at the same time; it is why there are never enough resources and why government is always too big. The 'common power' has grown flabby and ferocious: both absolute and inconstant, at once sterile and inefficient, sometimes servant and sometimes master.

Can we do better than this? The impulse to abstraction, the wish for a government or society whose mission is to obviate the home and detach the individual from their context, is strong. Most people's lives are limited to some degree by the unfair dispensation of wealth and opportunity. The human predicament is that almost everyone has a profound heart-cry for *something other than this*. The desire to escape, to reinvent, to defy one's birth and make a life somewhere else, is the essential staple of plot and character in English literature. Yet literature is the exception to the rule.

For all our longing for adventure, except at moments of angst or anguish, most people do not want a journey to elsewhere, a picaresque drama to find themselves or their fortune. Most people simply want the places they live in to be lovable: to be safe, healthy and beautiful, and to offer a good range of ordinary opportunities. And most people want their natural affections and loyalties to be honoured and endorsed, not despised, by the culture and the government.

Instead of a social contract, an imagined deal struck in the light of 'reason' between the sovereign individual and the totalising state, we need a social covenant. This word is difficult. Its origin is in the peace treaties and tribal agree-ments of the ancient Near East, adopted and adapted by the people who became Israel to explain their relationships with God and with each other, and in due course with the land they inhabited. It defines a model of political organisa-tion that is deep in the foundations of the West, and of the United Kingdom in particular. Put most simply, the politics of the covenant is built not on reason but on love.

The meaning of the word has been well conveyed by the phrase 'artificial brotherhood'.[7] A covenant is a way of expressing and formalising the love – unconditional, unstinting, permanent – that can exist between people who are unrelated by blood. The foundational social covenant is marriage, the union of two unrelated people that forms the nucleus of a new blood relationship, a family. Other cove-nants, less obvious and discrete, work in the same way.

Just as families are made by the covenant of marriage, so places – human communities situated in a geography – are made by the covenants of civil society, the formal and infor-mal institutions and associations through which the people of a neighbourhood achieve agency and belonging. Nations, meanwhile, are formed by the covenant of statehood, the mysterious complex of powers, ceremonies and institutions in which a people recognise, authorise and confess allegiance to their country.

In each of these covenants, something real is acknowl-edged: an elemental and important thing is honoured, made safe and put to a social purpose. The goal of the marriage covenant is to make *sex* safe – to reduce its capacity to wreck relationships and produce unwanted babies – making it the foundation of a family. The covenant of place, the local arrangement of civil society, honours the *land*, and makes on a patch of earth a community that regulates and, through local economic activity, sustains itself. And the covenant of statehood, in Burke's phrase, 'makes power gentle, and obedience liberal': it tames the fact of *violence*, the capacity of the strong to dominate the weak, and so creates a nation, which is something not merely to fear but to be loyal to, even to fight and die for.[8]

The covenants of family, place and nation share a set of qualities. Being rooted in physical reality – sex, land, violence – they reflect the nature of things, and thus transmit the ordinary affections that people feel towards their family, their neighbourhood and their country. Crucially, though, they create communities of difference. A covenant is essentially heterogeneous. This is true in marriage, where the partners come from different families and each bring their own identities and idiosyncrasies to the creation of this new thing. It is true in neighbourhoods, which are naturally diverse: as Andrew Rumsey has pointed out, the Greek *'paroikoi'*, the word from which we derive 'parish', means someone outside the household, a stranger to the people. The parish is a community of the unrelated, with an obligation to the outsider.[9] And the same goes for nations, or at least this nation. The British are bound by something quite other than blood; ours is a civic not a racial nationalism, an 'artificial brotherhood' forged by centuries of peaceful enjoyment of the common inheritance to which all newborn citizens, whether ethnic Saxons or Afghans, are equal heirs.

The heterogeneity of a covenant is resolved in a further quality. A covenant, unlike a contract, does not simply force competing interests into a legal arrangement by which each expects to profit, and in which each remains essentially an adversary. A covenant aligns interests, including the interests of those who are not direct parties to the arrangement, such as future generations or the natural world.

The essential difference between the 'social contract' we derive from Hobbes and Locke and the 'social covenant' we need is that the relations of a covenant have the quality not of choice but of givenness. A covenant is not created by your consent, but sustained by your assent. You join something that existed already – this is so even in marriage, where you join 'the married state' whose terms and conventions, and the very form of the ceremony that admits you to it, are laid down in advance. Indeed, even in marriage, where the relations begin in choice, the choice takes the form (at least in pretence) of an assent to the only choice that is really possible: a yielding to the compulsion of love.

The meaningful choice in all these covenants is not whether to enter but whether to leave them. You are always free to change your nationality, leave your neighbourhood or divorce your partner. But the expectation is that these are commitments that matter, and indeed they keep their hold on you even if you walk away. The covenant itself might be broken, but the thing it makes – the family, the community, the nation – endures, with you part of it. You can never entirely renounce the land and place of your birth, and a divorce does not cancel the responsibility you have to the person you once loved and promised to care for, and certainly not to the children you made together. A covenant is not conditional, like a contract, where one party can renege if the terms are broken. It is an 'artificial brotherhood'. Like a blood relationship, it cannot be undone, and where there is a permanent breach there is lifelong regret.

The covenant gives us a common conception of the good, a language in which we can understand each other and a sense of collective endeavour towards a better world which we can all imagine. And it gives to each individual the proper ground of personal freedom: it is the 'strong base', in the words of the child psychologist John Bowlby, for 'bold ventures'.[10]

What does the strong base look like in the twenty-first century? What are the proper objects of our collective endeavour? They are best expressed by a phrase of the economist Paul Collier: the 'equality of condition'.[11] Everyone should have a good upbringing and education, a secure home and a family of their own, the right help if misfortune or illness strikes, and a role to play in the world. These are the elements of a good life. And for most people they are to be found not by severing their relationships, 'liberating' them from the people and places they come from, but by making those people and places as healthy and virtuous as possible.

We have never had equality of condition in Britain. And so, partly perhaps in response to this long disappointment, we have broken the covenants that would yet produce it. The distresses and discontents in our society and economy follow from our disregard of the understandings that sustain families, neighbourhoods and the nation.

We have progressively diminished, to the point of abolition, the marriage covenant. We have reduced civic life, the covenant that holds communities together, to municipal maintenance, as if the only topic for the politics of a place were the collection of bins and the filling of potholes. And the national covenant is broken, or partly so. In the 1990s and 2000s, European treaties arrogated power and authority to Brussels. From 2004, the government authorised mass migration on a scale never before known in these islands. And a series of innovations in the constitution of the UK – the Human Rights Act and the Equality Act, devolution and the Supreme Court – unpicked the evolved conventions that had placed Parliament and the common law at the apex of the constitution.

Brexit represented a momentous declaration on the part of the country to restore the covenant between the people,

Parliament and the law. The great decision of 2016, ratified in the election of 2019, showed that the British people are capable of demanding profound change in the way they are governed. We need to fulfil the mandate of those votes, but we need to do much more than this.

I argue in this book that the purpose of politics is the cultivation of the conditions of virtue, of the moral impulses that make good conduct, and that these conditions are the normative dispositions of a conservative society.

A normative is a belief about reality, and an action in response. We believe things fall through the air, and therefore we are careful near clifftops. I argue that in political terms we have a mistaken normative, and we need to change it. The political normative we have is the belief that people are independent, infallible, moral creators, and that therefore the job of government is to facilitate their independence. The normative we need is the belief that people are dependent, fallible creatures, subject to a moral order, and yet capable of great goodness and achievement; therefore action is required to strengthen the institutions that mitigate our weakness and help us realise our potential.

'There is an objectively right way to be human,' as John Milbank plainly puts it, which is to say that individuals are happiest, and society is safest and most prosperous, when we conform to some fairly traditional habits.[12] This is the dispute we call the culture war. On one side are those self-styled 'progressives' who think that traditional normative dispositions are the source of the problem, and that dismantling them will deliver well-being, peace and safety from the system risks outlined above. On the other side are conservatives, like me, who think these dispositions reflect the truth of things, and that they therefore work as ways of living. We also believe that traditional habits are the best and only proper ground for freedom, tolerance and even – within proper limits – transgression. Without the conservative normative we will have Hobbes's 'war of all against all', and the inevitable ascent of some new, much darker normative that brooks no dissent or diversity whatever.

Progressives are of course right to point out the many injustices that exist today and existed even more in the days when traditional dispositions were dominant. But I suggest that the yearning for a more just, more free, more meaningful and moral society is a yearning for the past, that at heart the new Jerusalem is a reflection of the old one. Where, after all, do these ideas of justice and morality come from, if not from the submerged inheritance we receive from our history?

This is why, for all we are fighting a culture war, we are not fighting to the death. We are one country, one civilisation, with a common root, the classical Christian worldview that gave life to both conservatism and liberalism, the two great traditions that contest for power in our politics. The problem is that modern liberalism is the host to a parasite, a false and dangerous philosophy that has twisted our common inheritance into something untrue and bad. This false faith, not the progressives who profess it, is our enemy.

The culture war, as I argue in Chapter One, is a religious conflict about the right gods to worship. As such, it is more than a series of skirmishes for the tokens of identity, for flags and statues and the history curriculum. It is a battle for the strongholds of society itself, and for the future we are creating, or destroying, for our children.

There have always been critiques of Western civilisation from within, from parts of the elite dissatisfied with the ideas or the dispensations of power in society; dissent is indeed a vital mechanism for society's survival. But our culture has never before adopted the critique of itself as its governing philosophy. It is difficult to imagine how civilisation that essentially repudiates itself can possibly survive.

We – conservatives of left and right, all those who believe in the old way – need to win this battle, to restore the conservative normative as the proper basis for our culture and society, with a restored 'covenantal' understanding at the heart of families, neighbourhoods and the nation. We then need a new Elizabethan (or indeed Restoration or Hanoverian, or in the American context, Hamiltonian) settlement, a new version of that peculiarly English compromise that accommodates the defeated opponent and involves them in the task of creating the peace that follows.

Doing this well – the victory and the accommodation – could be the start of a great new age. Indeed, it is not too much to say that modernity could yet be the greatest possible blessing to the covenantal society; or, put another way, modernity will be a blessing to society so long as we restore the covenants that hold society together. For all the threats that beset us, and despite the conservative inclination to be gloomy about the future, there are great reasons to be cheerful. Tech can be tamed, and put to good service. Transgressive ideas can be corrected, and the impulse to change and progress channelled into courses that do good. The great irruption of innovation that our age is witnessing could yet make us safe, free and well, or as much of these things as is possible in a world that will never be perfect.

As I shall try to show in this book, late modernity is making a more traditional way of life possible again, and making the traditional way of life better: less brutal, more equal and more free. This is most obviously and importantly so in the foundational covenantal relationship. Marriage evolved in the Christian West at least partly as a means of giving women a distinct status, equal in honour and respect to men and protected from the dangers that single women faced in pre-modern society.

In practice, of course, the institution was widely abused, both in individual marriages by physically dominant men and in the general culture, which treated women as the property of men and marriage as a means of transferring ownership from the father to the husband. Yet marriage need not be – should never have been – like this. Marriage can and should be genuinely equal; indeed, it is the best means possible for realising the equality of the sexes, and modern life can make it so.

In the same way, the traditional settled communities to which most people aspire, but which in the old days were frequently stultifying, dismal and unjust places to live, can be revived by modernity. The internet is taking places (like Devizes, which I represent in Parliament) back to their pre-industrial glory, a place of multiple trades, crafts and the arts. The market town and village can be viable economic local centres once again, as they were before the rush to the cities, and city life can likewise resemble a more connected, more sustainable community, where neighbours know each other and share the common burdens and pleasures of a place. Modern communications and tech can help nations become what they ideally are, objects of loyalty within, and respect without: semi-autonomous, self-sufficient in the essentials and capable of repelling the aggression of others, but also part of a global community and connected particularly to other nations that share their values and customs.

These happy visions are uncontroversial. In all of them, however, there is a catch, or a cost. We cannot realise the original ideals of family, neighbourhood or nation without recognising that each of these things demands a sacrifice appropriate to its purpose.

To make marriage what it should be – an equal, enduring partnership – we have to acknowledge that its purpose is the regulation, the right ordering, of sexual relations; that in theory at least, and certainly according to the messages we should give our children, marriage is the safest and best place for sex.

To restore the covenant of place, the institutions of civil society, demands a sacrifice of time and effort by each of us to the neighbourhood that claims us; my suggestion is that everyone should perform 'council service' – a year as a part-time local councillor – at least once in their lives.

And the cost of nationhood, aside from the compulsions of tax-paying and law-abiding that are expected of the citizen, is deference to the past, and to the historic culture of these islands: within the natural constraints of a culture that does not go in much for boasting and flag-waving, and with full tolerance and respect for the many different cultures represented in our population, we need a more self-confident civic nationalism in public life.

The suggestions outlined here – supporting marriage, expecting people to serve their neighbourhoods, promoting patriotism – will seem ridiculous to some. But married, community-minded, patriotic people would find these sacrifices to be light burdens, and the effect therefore would be to make more people in that mould, which is what we need. For we are in a mighty battle, and only strong families, strong places and strong nations will prevail.

1

THE IDEA AND THE ORDER

THE CONDITIONS OF VIRTUE

You are what you worship. Your identity is a reflection of your god, the thing you venerate, which gives life meaning and explains good and evil. A culture is the act of common worship, and so a community or a civilisation might best be defined in terms of the gods the people serve.

To generalise crudely, pagan societies served the material world. They worshipped living creatures, wood and stone, the sea and stars, and imbued these physical things with spiritual properties. And they placed themselves in this world: human beings were subject to the mystical powers of animals, the land and the elements.

Judaism and Christianity restored the material world to itself, stripping out the hocus-pocus: animals and trees are just animals and trees. The object of worship was a great and singular god who made the universe. And this god, God, had a special place in his creation for human beings. We were not a subject of nature but its steward. We were given the Earth to look after, and were subject only to God himself.

Now, in our post-Christian age, what do we worship? We worship ourselves. We might think we worship nothing, just as we believe in nothing, or at least not in God. But as Bob Dylan knew, you gotta serve somebody. And we have decided to serve mankind, and more particularly the individual person, and even more particularly the person within: 'the real me'. Meanwhile, nature is disregarded, neither spiritualised nor stewarded, but rather plundered and abused.

In the modern era, meaning the last two or three hundred years, but especially the last twenty or thirty, the authority of a whole social order – of institutions, traditions and habits of thought, of social relations and obligations, of principles, practices, interests and affections – has been gradually replaced by the authority of something else. 'The Order' persists in fragments, as the remnants of a social system that is our only inheritance, but its authority is gone, or nearly, and so its fragments are disappearing too.

The Order was the arrangement of society around a common conception of the way to live, and around the practices of common worship. A culture whose god was outside the self created related and 'relational' beings. A person, we felt and thought in the old days, is a social animal. And so the Order organised the life of the individual to be 'other-facing': it stipulated and ensured that you lived for other people. My sense of myself derived from people other than me, with whom I was linked by the ties of love, service and dependence.

Thus the ordinary affiliations of life – families, communities and nations – were charged with the quality of the sacred. The holy mystery was reified, made material, not in wood and stone but in other people, and in the establishments of society: in homes, businesses, civic institutions, in the organisations of leisure and education and care, and in the state. These institutions were (at least in theory and sometimes in reality) easy-going within, generous and peaceable without, and plural by default. The mix of ages, sexes and functions in a household, of trades and responsibilities in a place, and of ideas, ethnicities and religions in a country, created relationships of like and unlike. All the pied beauty of humanity was held together by a common belief that beneath all and above all was something more important than any of it.

In the Order, the memberships and gathering places of communities mediated our differences and facilitated collective action. Membership and gathering were thought necessary because human beings are vulnerable and need the support and safety of the group, but also because human beings are greedy, and need the restraint and accountability of the group. In the Order, the function of society was to mitigate our vulnerability and greed, providing the support and restraint that individuals need to live well with one another.

Politics, as the business of the management of our common life, supported this function through deliberate action to strengthen the associations of society and thereby to strengthen us. Membership of a community was the context for the habits and skills that are the highest expressions of human capability. And in community, through iteration and testing, individuals discovered (rather than created) the rules of right and wrong.

To a conservative, the source of trouble in the world is not exterior but interior to human beings. The real meaning of freedom, as the concept has been understood from Aristotle onwards, is not freedom from the tyranny of others but freedom from the tyranny of ourselves. The true tyrant is our own caprice, the power of our appetites and our impulses to selfishness and self-harm.[1] Our passions forge our fetters.[*]

To defeat the tyrant caprice, to attain true freedom, we need virtue. The word is not to be understood in a drily moral sense. To be virtuous is not to be pinched, diminished and joyless. The virtues are the habits by which we cultivate the good life for ourselves and those around us. As Edward

---

[*] 'It is ordained in the eternal constitution of things, that men of intemperate minds cannot be free. Their passions forge their fetters.' Edmund Burke, 'Letter to a Member of the National Assembly', 1791.

Skidelsky puts it, they are 'the excellences of the species', the things humans are good at: 'they are to us what speed is to the leopard or strength to the lion'.[2] And as this suggests, the good life means more than a passive sense of well-being. It includes well-doing, the practice of 'excellences' like friendship, forbearance and overcoming – practices that make us our happiest and our best. And the practice of the virtues does not just make us personally happier, it makes life better for everyone else.

Virtue is a pre-Christian concept. To the ancients, the value of community was that it taught the individual loyalty, courage and self-sacrifice: the skills or habits that both protect the tribe and give a person the fullest expression of life. Into this tradition Christianity fitted like a hand in a glove. But first it turned the glove inside out. For the virtues of the ancients are the ingredients of success, the qualities of strength. Christianity supplemented them with the qualities of weakness, the ingredients of a society in which not everyone is strong.

To the martial virtues of the heroic tradition a new set was added: virtues like charity, temperance, continence, prudence, shrewdness, forgiveness, faith and humility. The words have a deadening Victorian ring to them now, yet they were and are radical. For they transformed the *telos* of society – the good life we aim towards – from one of attainment and success, with all that implied in terms of war and exploitation, to one of justice and peace.

THE BLACK HOLE

The proper purpose of politics is the cultivation of the conditions of virtue. These conditions are the Order: the arrangement of families, communities and nations which, at their best, make the best of us. They make more likely the production of good people.

Families, communities and nations persist, but they live on the diminishing legacy of principles we no longer uphold. The Order has given way to an idea, whose authority is the new power in our lives. 'The Idea' is simply this: that there exist autonomous agents, called individuals, who both self-determine and self-moralise. They decide for themselves who and what they are, and indeed what wider reality is, and they decide for themselves what is right and wrong. The Idea is that the individual, me myself, or more accurately the inner tyrant whom Aristotle warned us of, is the proper object of our worship.

The Idea is the oldest, the original mistake: that we can be like God, with our own creative power and the ability to decide for ourselves what is good and what is evil. The irony, of course, is that even this error takes succour from the Order it rejects. The great value of Christianity to Western culture, as Tom Holland has shown, is that it unpicked the total identification of the individual with the group.[3] Because for all that community gives the individual identity, it also creates manifold opportunities for the abuse of power. Christianity gave the person a different status from that given by society: a new status of being totally valuable, wholly unique and loved, with a worth deriving not from your tribe or social standing but from your existence as a child of God.

Over time – the lengthening time called the *saeculum* in which the world waited for the second coming of Christ – this principle of individual human dignity seeped into law and government: the Church developed 'secular' rules for the arbitration of disputes, which were duly adopted by chiefs and kings. In England, this blended with the common law, the evolving body of rulings that gave coherence and force to the customs that already prevailed among the people. In this way, with the sanction of the Church, the state came to protect society from itself, and to ensure that the poor and weak had some vestige of security against power. And so developed the greatest achievement of the West: the free man and woman.

It is important to remember the Christian basis of political liberty, because the creature has disavowed its creator. Liberty has repudiated its own origins. The individual, his God-given value recognised and protected in law, has decided in his pride that his freedom is his own achievement, that his power is his own – even, most absurdly, that he fought Christianity to be free.

For this we can blame the eighteenth century. In Britain and Europe at this time, the late medieval distrust of abstract universal claims about knowledge or existence became a more hostile antagonism towards mystery, revelation and religion itself. The hunt was on for a set of principles to govern human society, founded on solid ground: rules that could be seen and proved to be true. The paradox is that the search for solid ground led not to a sensible earthly reality, but to the upper air. For the scientific method applied to questions of right and wrong becomes a vortex of abstraction. In the light of the Enlightenment, everything real or established, any accepted beliefs, anything that people felt or knew to be true, became suspect. Validity had to be conferred according to a new revelation: the logic that proceeds from the minds of intellectuals. Yet no intellectual is safe from his or her successor.

Political, moral and social theory in the West had previously developed progressively, with new generations building upon and modifying the inheritance of their forbears, and all respecting the common root of classical, Jewish and Christian ideas. After the eighteenth century, the process was reversed, and as 'progress' became the spirit of the age in science and technology, social and moral thought went into regress.

By the mid-nineteenth century, Karl Marx was denying any forward or progressive energy in society except want and greed. Soon, Friedrich Nietzsche denied even this idea of progress. There is certainly no God, Nietzsche said, but nor is there anything else, not even the logic of materialism. And so the Enlightenment project to find a rational morality came in the end, which happened quite quickly, to this: a madman in the marketplace, screaming that there is no hope. The catastrophe of the two world wars seemed to prove Nietzsche right.[4]

The Idea began, then, in the exaggerated rationalism of the Enlightenment, in a hubristic confidence in the ability of the mind of man to free itself of prejudice and historical baggage and work out the meaning of things. Yet the failure of the Enlightenment, first in philosophic nihilism and then in the immolation of the trenches and the gas chambers, was the real occasion for the Idea to step forth. In the mid-twentieth century, the failed project to invent or discover a singular rational morality – the project we might call political modernism – yielded gradually to political postmodernism: the right of each person to invent or discover a morality of their own. This time, the Idea was the property not of intellectuals but of each of us. 'You are free,' said Jean-Paul Sartre. 'Therefore choose.'*

Sartre famously summarised his philosophy with the dictum 'existence precedes essence'. He thought that the fact of being is entirely neutral: we enter the world with no identity or obligation, no 'essence': we are free – indeed we are obliged, and this is the only obligation we have – to fashion our own essence. There is no objectively right way

---

* 'You are free, therefore choose, that is to say, invent. No rule of general morality can show you what you ought to do: no signs are vouchsafed in this world.' Jean-Paul Sartre, *Existentialism Is a Humanism*, (Methuen, 1946).

to be human, only the subjective imperative to make it up for ourselves. 'The Idea' is the idea that I am God, with the power, the right and the responsibility to make the world the way I want it.*

The original eighteenth-century revolution against the Order was wrong but at least – like the founding fathers of the Hamiltonian party in America, who held to the idea of a monarchy-like government – the revolutionaries attempted to replicate artificially the system they had overthrown: a singular unifying concept of truth. The greater offence followed, although we could say it was inevitable once the Order had been overthrown: the overthrow of its replica, the alternative, botched-together singular truth, in favour of a billion personal truths all claiming the status of the absolute.

The transition was not immediate or obvious. Sartre's utter repudiation of Enlightenment liberalism was seen rather as its natural and beneficent evolution. Throughout the late twentieth century, and even today, liberals earnestly believed that in throwing to the four winds the concept of a singular morality they were extending liberty. Instead they were hastening its demise, and their own too.

---

* '[I]f God does not exist there is at least one being whose existence comes before its essence, a being which exists before it can be defined by any conception of it. That being is man... Man first of all exists, encounters himself, surges up in the world – and defines himself afterwards... To begin with he is nothing. He will not be anything until later, and then he will be what he makes of himself... Man is nothing else but that which he makes of himself.' *Ibid.*

Sartre's essay was published in 1946. It was not until 2020 that his principles became official doctrine. This was the year, as Yoram Hazony explains, when staff at the *New York Times*, the house journal of American liberalism, prevailed on the editor to fire a group of senior colleagues *because they were liberal* – because they wrote in defence of the old idea that there is such a thing as truth independent of people's feelings.[5]

It was in 2020 that the Idea took over. Having killed liberalism from within, it has animated its carcase with a different philosophy, and this zombified monster now rules instead. What shall we call it? I find 'woke' too trivial, too mocking for such a powerful and resourceful enemy. 'Cultural Marxism' works, for it refers to a comparable theory with the same analysis (the inherent hostility of groups, here translated from the economic to the cultural sphere) and the same revolutionary spirit.

But a simpler name might be 'transgressive'. For the new doctrine has no theory of change, as Marxism does, no account of the dynamic interactions of interests bar the confusions of 'intersectionality' (the pretence that the inevitable clash of competing identities in the hierarchy of grievance is some vindication of a politics built on grievance, rather than, as should be obvious, evidence of the absurdity of such a politics). All the new doctrine has is the Idea, the principle that nothing matters except the dominant individual will. By this doctrine, the sole impulse of individuals, the only thing that gives them purpose and coherence, is to repudiate their inheritance and transgress the norms expected of them.

In replacing the Order with the Idea we replace the centrality of relationships with the centrality of the self. The culture no longer expects us to live for others, and we no longer expect to be fulfilled through our memberships: we live for ourselves, and we expect to be fulfilled by the realisation of some personal goal. This goal might involve other people – to have a family or a particular career – but the others have become means to our happiness, not ends in themselves. And we ourselves are not fulfilled in the process, but broken. For *contra* Sartre, we are not free, or at least not free from the impulse to worship. We were born to worship: this is our essence, as primary as our existence.

The repudiation of an exterior god directs our worship inwards. Self-worship dislocates the relationship of subject and object, worshipper and worshipped, by making them the same thing. The effect is an awful psychic split, as part of ourselves – some inward, 'authentic' part – now fills the space once filled by divinity. Hence our distress. Traditionally, we knew ourselves to be uniquely significant, fully valuable for ourselves alone, but also part of a general body or bodies: the subdivisions of families, communities and nations.

We were partakers of a universal and public philosophy that honoured both individual uniqueness and corporate membership. Now the public philosophy is transgressive gnosticism, the worship of incorporeal wisdom, to be gained by an inner truth-seeking available only to a few. Only those, indeed, who have found within themselves some identity that sets them apart from the mainstream, that puts them at odds with the culture of their inheritance, are thought to have attained the gnosis, the secret wisdom of the world. And the secret is simply this: that I am perfect, and you are not.

In the Order, the only problem is me. I am fallible, and selfish, and dim-sighted. And the job of society is to mitigate this problem, helping me be better and protecting others from my mistakes. In the world of the Idea, by contrast, I am pure and innocent, and the problem therefore lies elsewhere: in creation, and in others. In the world of the Idea the enemy is other people.

This is difficult to reconcile with the professions of tolerance and diversity that characterise the new regime. Yet the new regime is clothed in the garb of the host, liberalism, whom it has poisoned. The Idea begins with a universal blandness – the stripping away of anything personal or particular, the renunciation of any given identity or loyalty outside the self – and proceeds to a vicious factionalism.

As Alistair McFadyen puts it, 'anything really particular becomes pathological'.[6] A happy society is an association of people with something in common, something outside themselves as individuals: a society of self-determining, self-moralising individuals is one where the only thing held in common is humanity itself. And when you have concluded that the problem lies in other people, this is no adhesive at all.

The Order entails diversity within a common culture. The Idea undoes this. Instead of the connections between like and unlike, we develop exclusive identities of interest and ideology. Differences become a source of offence, and a contest of power, of who has aggrieved whom. We struggle to live together. Our particular features stripped away, our personal morality amplified in the vacuum of infinite space, we are a society of shrieking ghosts, colourless harridans, and no less harmful for being ghostly. For a scheme of moral autonomy, the right of everyone to inhabit their own moral universe does not lead to a society of tolerance.

Each individual's personal moral scheme has no common ground with anyone else's. I report from my universe to yours. Moral debate, which hardly deserves the name, becomes the shouting of rival theories, each rooted in no deeper soil than one person's feeling or belief. For each universe has imperial ambitions. My only relationship with you is one of mutual attempted exploitation and domination. Self-expression, as MacIntyre says, becomes simply 'the attempt of one will to align the choices of another with its own'.[7] And so it is that the vocabulary of liberty, of 'be yourself' and 'live and let live' leads, despite itself, to conformity and enmity, to an in-group intolerant of eccentricity and viciously hostile to out-groups.

Of course, the Idea is rarely confessed. No one admits that the enemy is other people, or proudly declares their wish to subjugate everyone else to their own absolutist worldview. But the wish is evident in what they say. Like a black hole, the Idea is known by its effects on surrounding objects. It is the dark presence that draws the moral universe towards itself, and so steadily reduces everything to nothing.

The principle of personal dignity and individual value becomes 'I don't care what people think'. The idea of freedom becomes 'I can do whatever I want', and indeed 'others must help me do it'. The great gift of individual uniqueness becomes 'I am whatever I want to be'. The fact of emotions, of all their power to move, becomes 'my feelings matter above all else', and the fact of our emotional vulnerability becomes 'I must be protected from the words and thoughts of others'. Yet these trite and selfish statements run up against our own deeper knowledge of the way things actually are.

The Idea denies all that in our hearts and minds we know to be true about ourselves. We know we inherit capabilities and dispositions from our parents and distant ancestors, yet the Idea dismisses genetics in favour of a blank slate at birth. We know we are also made of our experiences, that our attitudes are conditioned by life, yet the Idea says we are objective and rational beings who can exclude everything personal and particular from our thinking. We know that we want to belong, that we love most the people closest to us, that our deepest impulse is for human connection, yet the Idea pretends that our wish is really for unfettered independence and that we have equal obligations to all of humanity (which is equivalent to saying we have no obligations to anyone).

Most of all, perhaps, we know things are awry at heart. Life is somehow faulty, and even our experiences of joy or beauty have the quality of loss or yearning. Happiness is like an echo, or a foretaste, a glimpse of things as they should be but are not. Art understands this, or did. It told stories of virtue, of people struggling for the better world from which we feel ourselves to be exiled, and failing, but in the struggle gaining something of the prize.*

The Idea denies that things are awry at heart; all that is wrong, according to the Idea, is the social and economic system created by abusive elites and the wrong-think or 'false consciousness' that this system has induced in the public. This singular and simple story replaces the stories – plural, rich and strange – of the Order. Instead of tales of virtue amid defeat, of men and women on the long journey home, we have the grim narrative of progress. In this story the future looks like the present, only better, because it will

---

* Referring to his famous sentence in *The Lord of the Rings*, 'we have fought the long defeat', Tolkien later wrote in a letter, 'I do not expect "history" to be anything but a "long defeat" – though it contains (and in a legend may contain more clearly and movingly) some samples or glimpses of final victory.' This is very English, as Orwell would have recognised: our literature celebrates defeats and retreats as the occasions of heroism that tell of a greater triumph. 'The most stirring battle-poem in English is about a brigade of cavalry which charged in the wrong direction.' George Orwell, 'England Your England', *The Lion and the Unicorn: Socialism and the English* (Genius Secker & Warburg, 1941).

finally be free of all residual prejudice and superstition: because the old stories will finally be forgotten. Power will finally arrange itself for social justice. We will have, in the words of T.S. Eliot, 'systems so perfect that nobody needs to be good'.[8]

Already in place of enchanted realism we have the disenchanted lie. Rather than the truth decked in romance and mystery, we have a falsehood, presented plain. In the Order, reality is made fabulous in the public art and in the stories and histories by which we honour ourselves and our ancestors: in style and dress and ritual, by all the charming exaggerations and contradictions with which we buff and polish the truth to make the light dance around it.

The lie has no such innocent tricks of presentation, no pleasing art to beguile us into loyalty to the way things are and should be. The lie lives its fabulous life within, at the level of the inner man or woman: 'the real me'. For there some dark magic may be performed. Down there proper alchemy that can turn one person into another is possible – where reality itself is fluid and whatever is hoped for becomes true.

THE LAWS OF THE IDEA

The rest of this book is an attempt to challenge the workings of the Idea and to find ways to restore the Order it has nearly destroyed. This restoration is primarily a job for culture – for our ideas and habits in private and civil life – and for public administration, including fiscal policy and the organisation of the state. But above and beneath these ordinary domains is a quasi-constitutional legal architecture that is itself the product of the Idea and which will make it difficult for culture and public administration to reform in the ways that are necessary. This architecture consists primarily of two pieces of legislation that book-ended the Blair-Brown governments: the Human Rights Act of 1998 and the Equality Act of 2010.

Both these laws have admirable intentions and indeed derive from earlier codes that reflected English legal traditions. It may be that future applications of them, their interpretation by future judges, can return us to these traditions, if the wider political and cultural context shifts back towards sanity. But the Human Rights Act and the Equality Act show in the text and in their workings the pull of the black hole of the Idea. They represent the construction of systems designed to make goodness redundant.

The Human Rights Act incorporated into domestic UK law the 1950 European Convention of Human Rights (ECHR), requiring British courts to apply the provisions of the Convention as if they were British laws. And in a sense they were, for the Convention was drafted with the help of British (indeed Conservative) lawyers in the aftermath of World War II, who deliberately sought to bring to Europe the tradition of English liberty. Before 1998, UK citizens could only appeal for their Convention rights to the European Court of Human Rights in Strasbourg, a lengthy and expensive process. The Human Rights Act, in the words of Tony Blair, 'brought rights home'.

But what sort of rights? In 1950, the countries of Europe pledged themselves against torture and extra-judicial killing, and for freedom of speech and the rule of law. These principles had of course been enshrined in English common law for centuries, and initially the government thought it unnecessary for the UK to join the Convention itself. European fellow-feeling prevailed, however, and we signed up.[9]

The basic rights encoded in the ECHR have been supplemented over time, not through new articles to the Convention agreed by national governments, but by means of what is called 'evolutive interpretation', which rests on the claim by the Strasbourg Court that the Convention itself is a 'living instrument'. The Human Rights Act incorporates into British law not just the original 1950 text of the ECHR but all the judgements made in Strasbourg ever since, including since the Act supposedly 'brought rights home' in 1998. The Human Rights Act thus represents not only a foreign import, but an understanding of rights that long ago left the ordinary ground laid by those British Conservative lawyers in the aftermath of World War II.

As the former Supreme Court judge Jonathan Sumption put it, the Court has developed the Convention 'by a process of extrapolation or analogy' to reflect modern ideas of the rights that citizens need.[10] This is most apparent in the application of Article 8 of the Convention, which asserts the right to private and family life. Article 8 was originally drafted to defend the right to marry and the privacy of the home. But it has become a catch-all power which blasts through every other area of law. As Sumption explains, areas considered justiciable by Strasbourg under 'the right to private and family life' include

> the legal status of illegitimate children, immigration and deportation, extradition, criminal sentencing, the recording of crime, abortion, artificial insemination, homosexuality and same sex unions, child abduction, the policing of public demonstrations, employment and social security rights, environmental and planning law, noise abatement, eviction for non-payment of rent and a great deal else besides. All of these things have been held to be encompassed in the protection of private and family life. None of them is to be found in the language of the convention. None of them is a natural implication from its terms. None of them has been agreed by the signatory states. They are all extensions of the text which rest on the sole authority of the Judges of the Strasbourg Court. This is, in reality, a form of non-consensual legislation.[11]

In Sumption's words, 'the Strasbourg Court has developed [Article 8] into what it calls a principle of personal autonomy'. By these means, the sanctity of family life, the respect for the social form that reflects the most essential *constraint* on personal autonomy, becomes its vehicle and enabler. The institution that more than any other defines the individual for them, without their say-so, is deployed to make the argument that the sovereign individual has the right to absolute self-definition. The essential institution of the Order becomes the agent of the Idea.

This is the doctrine of the law that is effectively supreme in the British constitution. For the Human Rights Act is exempt from the doctrine of 'implied repeal' by which new laws have the effect of repealing earlier ones that contradict them. (Until Brexit, the 1972 European Communities Act was similarly exempt from implied repeal. Now only the Human Rights Act has this status of being sovereign and permanent – the equivalent of a constitutional document – in UK law.[12]) And not only is it immune from all subsequent laws. It gives judges the power to amend earlier legislation to suit its doctrines.

The ordinary function of English courts is to interpret legislation and precedent to give effect to the intentions of law-makers and maintain continuity of principle over time, so that all change is gradual and coherent. Yet British courts may, in the words of one judgement, 'read in words' – that is, alter the text – 'which change the meaning of enacted legislation, so as to make it Convention compliant... [thus] a court can modify the meaning, and hence the effect, of... legislation'.[13]

And even this is not the limit of the authority of judges to make the law. The Convention gives national courts a 'margin of appreciation' to interpret it in ways suitable to their particular country. Rather than using the margin of appreciation to *limit* the impact of the Convention on the United Kingdom, our courts have sometimes chosen to use it in the opposite way, to go 'further than Strasbourg'. Baroness Hale, sometime President of the Supreme Court of the UK, and others have argued that a UK court may find the government or other agencies to be in breach of Convention rights even if Strasbourg itself does not.[14] Thus the Act is both sovereign in UK law and almost infinitely elastic.

Rights, as Roger Scruton wrote, are not 'claims against others… To think of human rights in this way is to fill the world with vague and unfulfillable obligations, and therefore with vast and irresoluble conflicts'.[15] Rights, properly conceived, are simply the qualities we regard as sacrosanct to the person, which must not be invaded by others or by the state – namely one's life, liberty and property. We have these things as citizens, irrespective of our identity or affiliations. Rights are genuinely individualistic: they really do disregard one's particular characteristics or memberships, and they apply to you and me as undifferentiated equal units.

Yet the other great Act of the last Labour government changed this. The Equality Act 2010 created a set of rights for certain people based on their group identities. It identified a set of 'characteristics' that henceforth would be 'protected' by the law against discrimination by others. As with the Human Rights Act, the Equality Act was based on an existing legal framework that reflected a more traditional view of things. In this case, the inspiration was the Race Relations Act of 1976. The 1976 Act imposed a duty on public agencies to 'eliminate unlawful racial discrimination' in the performance of their functions and to 'promote... good relations, between persons of different racial groups'.

The duty involved the state in a positive moral good: to strive to ensure that people from ethnic minorities were not deliberately disadvantaged in the workings of the public sector. Importantly, therefore, the Act reflected a reactive conception of human rights, as things to be defended when a breach occurs. It assumed that in a well-ordered society people would behave well towards each other – that the essential structures of society were sound but, given the stresses introduced to British society by large-scale immigration, they required vigilance and reinforcement.

The concern of the Race Relations Act was evident in its title. It sought to ensure good relations between citizens. Over time, a thicket of more than a hundred additional laws grew up, each designed to address one or other injustice or disadvantage faced by different groups, such as people with disabilities or those in sexual minorities. It was these laws that were eventually consolidated in the Equality Act in 2010. And in the process something changed. The concern with 'relations' disappeared, to be replaced with the singular focus on 'equality'. The assumption of soundness – that the structures of society were ordered aright, and only breaches needed policing – was reversed. The state now holds that the structures of society are unsound. The problem is not individual cases of discrimination but 'systemic' bias, which it is the job of the state and its agencies – what the Act calls the 'Public Sector Equality Duty' – to eliminate.

Insofar as it simply consolidates previous anti-discrimination laws and therefore attempts to remove some of the 'vast and irresoluble conflicts' between them, the Equality Act may be said to be neutral or even benign in its effect. But as Bob Hepple has written, the real effect of the Act has been to introduce a new doctrine, which he calls 'transformative equality', into the law and into the practice of the state and its satellite agencies. This doctrine, Hepple says, is tantamount to a 'reinvention' of the legal basis on which matters of interpersonal conduct once stood.[16]

Formerly, the law insisted that people were treated equally, irrespective of their characteristics; now it insists on different treatment for different people. Formerly, the only identity the law recognised apart from one's citizenship, the only relationship that had relevance to the state, was the relationship of marriage, which gave one a special status with special rights and responsibilities. Under the Equality Act, the only 'protected characteristic' to which the Public Sector Equality Duty does *not* fully apply is marriage.[17]

Formerly, the law was blind; now it claims a penetrating perspicacity, the ability to peer into people's souls, discern any prejudices, and rectify them. To truly promote equality it has become necessary to police thoughts and feelings: to engineer attitudes and beliefs through the eradication of 'unconscious bias', and to control the environment that people with protected characteristics experience so as to minimise their exposure to hurtful behaviour. As the Equalities Minister Kemi Badenoch has said, the Act is too often used not as 'a shield' against prejudice, but as a 'sword' to prosecute the suspects of thought crime.[18]

It is frequently protested that all this is exaggerated. Certainly many judges and public servants are sensible, and resist the full logic of the legislation that they are required to apply. Yet like the ECHR and the Human Rights Act, the Equality Act has created the opportunity for far more drastic action in the future. The absurd and rare cases that agitate sections of Parliament and the media (and are usually overturned when sense prevails) are omens, harbingers of what is coming on a more general basis.

As the culture war heats up, the statutes and precedents are there to crush the defence of the Order, and we see plainly that there will be police and judges who would use them. In 2019, a British judge concluded that the view that a transgender woman is biologically male – that men are not women, in short – is a view that is 'not worthy of respect in a democratic society'.[19] In 2022, a woman was arrested for praying silently, on her own, in the street, by police enforcing a law which for the first time in modern British history bans not action or even speech but *thought*.[20]

As this suggests, even without the operation of the courts and the police, the new legal framework is effective through the voluntary action of people with power in their spheres. Firms and public sector bodies take it upon themselves to hire only people with what Paul Yowell calls 'a preferred set of moral sympathies and political opinions'.[21] Companies that control the means of public discourse, particularly the tech platforms that host our online lives, think it proper to use their power for the cause of transformative equality. In 2022, Paypal suspended the accounts of organisations – including one, ironically, dedicated to defending free speech – that give platforms to people who have heretical opinions on sex and gender, climate change and the response to Covid-19.

The leadership of our public and private sectors has collectively adopted the view that the foundations of society are rotten and illegitimate. Thus our leaders are transgressive, politically opposed to the mores of the people they lead. And their sons and daughters will be more so. The Marxist philosopher Herbert Marcuse argued, in a 1965 essay titled 'Repressive Tolerance', for 'the withdrawal of toleration of speech and assembly' from people who uphold conservative ideas. 'The restoration of freedom of thought,' said Marcuse, 'may necessitate new and rigid restrictions on teaching and practice in the educational institutions.'

The educational institutions are imposing these restrictions on themselves, in fear of a student body that has been radicalised to madness by the logic of the Idea. For if you believe that your identity, your very being, is how you feel, then the experience of hurt or offence is catastrophic. In this alternative reality, words are worse than sticks or stones: opinions that threaten a person's sense of themselves are blasphemy, sedition, not to be tolerated.

According to the Idea, the enemy is not within each of us, but out there: it is other people, and society itself. And thus the whole order of truth – of history, literature, even science, of all that is taught by one generation to the next – must wheel around and tack to the new wind. Thus universities, founded in tradition (the transmission of inherited knowledge) and reason (the constant fearless testing of that knowledge in the light of new insights), are under sustained attack. Both the accumulation of historic knowledge and the idea of free enquiry, with the free speech this entails, are invalidated by an ideology that denies any legitimacy to what simply *is*.

The law is a teacher: it is not simply by the direct effect of statute, as applied by judges in individual cases, that the law exerts its influence, but far more by the indirect effect of anticipatory compliance that it creates among people with power and influence who need to maintain or maximise their status. This is why the governing principles of the law, the theories or doctrines that it rests upon, are so important.

We need a better framework for our rights and liberties than the Human Rights Act and the Equality Act. We need a restoration of the principle that the rights of the British people are protected by the ordinary laws of the land.

The ECHR, the Human Rights Act and the Equality Act should be amended, or simply replaced with the simple assertions contained in the 1951 Convention and indeed in many preceding statutes in the English law: that the state shall protect the life, liberty and property of its citizens, and not interfere with them itself without due process. The real nature of rights is not 'claims against others' but the proper attributes of an individual in a community, with obligations that precede his or her independence: obligations to family, neighbourhood and nation. For all that rights apply to us equally, without reference to our affiliations, for this very reason they are mutual obligations: not claims made by one person or group against each other but shared responsibilities that bring benefits as well as duties.

Our rights properly consist of legal protections against interference (by government or by others) in the fulfilment of our obligations. To fulfil these obligations we need protection against false imprisonment, theft or mistreatment; we need the freedom to speak, assemble and worship according to our inclination and conscience; we need the ability to marry and to raise a family, and to direct the education of our children; and we need the right to a trial by jury, overseen by judges who only follow statute and precedent, applying the law as they believe it to be, not as they believe it *should* be. And in the modern age, we need protections against the 'technium', the security state, equipped and assisted by the industries of data and digital which offer such opportunities but also threaten the loss of freedom, of relationships and of human purpose.

All these rights can be asserted and claimed without reference to international law and without subjection to a foreign court. Yet this is not to repatriate morality, to make the relativist claim that every country can invent its own ideas of right and wrong. The whole legal order of Europe, including that of the United Kingdom, evolved as the expression of a universal moral scheme, to which governments and courts claimed obedience. The doctrine of human rights is of course a modern reflection of the universal scheme, but it is sadly corrupted by the claims of an alternative source – the authority of individual reason – and an alternative objective: not civil peace but individual self-realisation. We now turn to the fullest expression of this objective.

2

ON SEX AND DEATH

THE REGULATION OF SEX

I have suggested that the spirit of the law expressed in the application of the Human Rights Act and the Equality Act reflects a mistaken understanding of what makes for a good society. These Acts, and their supporters, are nevertheless determinedly decent; indeed, support for these Acts and everything they stand for is as clear a proxy for morality as churchgoing was in the nineteenth century. How have we arrived here, where to be moral is to be – in effect – transgressive?

Jonathan Haidt has the answer, although he does not follow his own argument quite to this conclusion. In *The Righteous Mind*, Haidt explains how the moral system of the West, and consequently its conversations about society, have shrunk to the two basic principles – what he calls 'moral foundations' – of 'care' and 'fairness'. These are the idea that we should be compassionate towards individuals who are suffering or disadvantaged, and the idea that we should allocate resources and opportunities across society on some fair principle. On our way through modernity we have lost sight of three other moral foundations, common to traditional societies, which are necessary to an individual's thought and to what sociologists call praxis: the habits of the community. The missing three foundations are authority, loyalty and sanctity.[1]

Authority is attachment to institutions and particularly to institutions that transmit expectations of behaviour, with or without the threat of coercion. It explains why most people respect the army, not for the soldiers' power but for their virtue, for the example they set of how to behave well.

Loyalty is attachment to place, nation and tribe. It explains why David Goodhart's anecdote in *The Road to Somewhere*, of sitting between the head of the civil service and the head of the BBC at an Oxford dinner and finding that they both agreed that British public policy should promote the global good, not the national interest, is so offensive to the ordinary British voter.[2]

Sanctity is reverence and awe at what is made, what is holy, like the human body or the natural world. It explains why people hate litter, and why the sight of someone with an ugly facial tattoo displeases us: because it violates something that is precious to all. Taken together, these principles explain why John Lennon's song 'Imagine' – with its wish for nothing to be loyal to, nothing authoritative, nothing sacred – is so dreary and so appalling.

Care and fairness are necessary moral foundations because they check the potential for abuse in the other three. They are, indeed, akin to the Christian virtues that came to supplement and soften the pagan ones. Authority, loyalty and sanctity can endorse and encourage terrible injustices, in which the individual person is sacrificed (even literally) to the dark gods of a tradition. The role of care and fairness is to challenge negative aspects of how things are, to correct the excesses that occur in any arrangement of human beings. But the other three foundations are also the sources of our happiness and safety, because they create the ties that bind us to each other. Together, the five foundations underpin the Order, a social arrangement in which the individual is happily subsumed but also protected against abuse.

When care and fairness are our only moral ideas, we have the Idea, not the Order: a morality of individual rights only. And this explains the poverty of our politics. We are reduced to a dispute, simultaneously technical and impassioned, about the effective administration of provision (care) and allocation (fairness). We argue, both sentimentally and aggressively, over production and distribution, using the thin vocabulary of utility, efficiency and choice, of cost and benefit. We have lost the language of human relations: words like love and affection, reciprocity and respect, generosity and justice – the language of authority, loyalty and sanctity. The fact that these words do not translate easily into 'policy', that they are hard to legislate into being, should not be held against them. We don't need more rules; we need habits of right living, to arrange our relationships for peace and prosperity.

This chapter attempts a defence of some very traditional principles – so traditional as to be widely scorned and almost universally ignored. It also warns against some very dark ideas that are gaining currency in the culture and in politics. In these topics, I suggest, is the deep battle between the Idea and the Order, and here are the real foundations of conservatism: the source of the covenants that society needs for its life.

Conservatism is a philosophy of sex and death. It has a view on the right regulation of these ultimate things, the things that make and unmake us. Indeed, all politics might be said to come down to the regulation of sex and death. Conservatism is more honest because it acknowledges quite openly that they are matters of public concern.

It used to be understood that the arrangement of social relations in a community derives from the regulation of sexual relations. The regulation of sex was central to public ritual, formalised and celebrated through religious ceremony and in the public art. The Anglican marriage service, with its explicit reference to 'the hallowing and right direction of the natural instincts and affections', placed sex at the heart and the start of a couple's official existence. And the generation and regulation of sexual energy were the subject of our best stories, the heady dramas of courting and mating and the tales of betrayal and lost or unrequited love. The regulation was crucial, just as the 'sprung rhythm' of Gerald Manley Hopkins's poetry laced his exuberant fecundity ('what is all this juice and all this joy?') into the form of a sonnet, and thus increased its power.

The traditional regulation of sex through the covenantal institution of marriage has the quality of a fairy-tale. On the face of it, marriage is an almost impossible undertaking. Its impossibility is best shown by imagining we were designing it today. Imagine if we created a template agreement that couples could sign up to: a voluntarily entered but binding commitment to sleep together, and not to sleep with anyone else, for the rest of their lives. Imagine furthermore that both parties pledged to pool their assets and their income, and to support each other (and their children and their parents as they age) through thick and thin – in short, to help and respect each other no matter what.

Imagine if signing this pledge was the only way you could get to have sex at all, or at least without doing it in secret: by finding someone willing to be faithful and respectful to you, and promising to be so to them. And then imagine your family and friends, and the rest of society, and the state itself, gathering round to recognise and celebrate your agreement, and pledging to provide help and respect to the pair of you.

The suggestion is, of course, preposterous. Put like this, it seems unimaginable that marriage as an institution can last much longer, so completely opposed are its obligations to the spirit of the age. And yet marriage remains the golden thread of our culture. The permanent settlement, 'happily ever after', is still the goal of romance. Indeed, what else could be? A restless seeking for satisfaction may provide life's most exciting dramas, but as our hearts know, the destination and purpose of it all is to find one person to dedicate yourself to, and to receive their dedication in turn. Nothing else will do, strange and difficult as it seems, and often unsatisfactory as it is in practice, especially if we forget that the wedding is not the end of the drama but its real beginning.

In the scheme of the virtues we are cast against type. Men and women seem naturally disposed to traits of wrongdoing over-represented among their sex and familiar from literature down the ages: male violence, for instance, or female jealousy. Yet marriage inverts these stereotypes. It assigns us nobler characters, edifying myths of what men and women could be, and which in heroic emulation we sometimes are: the supportive and respectful man, the loving and generous woman.

Marriage, like all covenants, is artificial: it realises an ideal; yet it suits us because it also reflects the way things are. Most of all, it recognises the fact of difference and of complementarity between the sexes. Same-sex marriage, legal in the UK since 2013, does not invalidate this principle, nor does the principle invalidate same-sex marriage: all marriages, gay and straight, involve the union of difference. Yet the origin of marriage, as the union of the sexes, represents the first and foundational expression in human social organisation of the diversity and the connectedness of the created order. The fundamental difference between men and women is both maintained and overcome by marriage: the difference is both honoured and made less salient, and so made safe.

In allying with our opposites, we bind the world together, reconciling, while recognising, the only real division that exists within humanity. Applied across society, marriage thus both separates and connects the sexes, holding them distinct but related, like two sets of parallel ropes laid upon each other at right angles and tied with knots where they meet: making a net.

I argued in the Introduction that a covenant takes something real and elemental, honours it and ensures it serves a social end. Marriage is the covenant of sex. It takes the most powerful, productive and potentially – because of its appeal – destructive force in human life and puts it to use, conferring benefits both material and social on the people who sign up to it. Yet, marvellously, it does this without making sex utilitarian, and in a way that respects privacy.

Marriage is built around baby-making, yet that is not its only purpose and certainly not its only benefit; nor is there some special value in the marriages that make babies, which other marriages lack. Marriage is the most liberal form of sexual regulation possible. It assumes sex, for instance in the way a woman's husband has 'assumed paternity' of her child, just as it assumes mutual commitment; the piece of paper denoting marriage means the state does not need to pry into living arrangements to test commitment or indeed into the DNA of a child to determine its parentage. The alternative, a system that gives the privileges of marriage to any couple, must either be gullible and much deceived, or offensively intrusive.*

If marriage blesses the adults who marry, it blesses their children just as much. For while there are countless examples of bad marriages, and of successful happy children brought up outside marriage, the evidence is overwhelming that marriage generally does what it is supposed to do: help couples stay together and bring up their children well. And the general effect of multiple marriages is to create a net that supports everyone. A society with a lot of marriage is strong enough to support everyone else, the individuals, couples and families whose lives, for whatever reason, do not fit the traditional pattern.

---

* The government's advice to front-line staff assessing benefits for unmarried couples starts with the statement 'couples, be they married or unmarried, should be treated in a similar way'. It then runs to fifteen pages to help a benefits decision-maker understand whether a couple meets the 'Living Together as a Married Couple (LTAMC)' test, including whether or not they are in a sexual relationship and whether the relationship 'has the emotional quality that characterises a married couple's partnership'. 'Universal Credit – Living together as a married couple', Department for Work and Pensions guidance.

THE DISMANTLING OF MARRIAGE

Marriage is normative: which is to say, it has or had a special status as the default arrangement for adult life and, crucially, for producing children. Other normatives are possible, however, aside from the light-touch sexual regulation that marriage entails. Two alternatives are familiar: over-regulation and no regulation. They are equally bad. In fear of the former we have chosen the latter.

The over-regulation of sex was the dark fantasy of twentieth-century progressive novelists, from George Orwell's communist dystopia *1984*, in which men and women are assigned to each other and expected to have sex as 'our duty to the party', to Margaret Atwood's *The Handmaid's Tale*, in which extreme religious conservatism forces women to make babies for the Republic of Gilead.

Orwell and Atwood wrote in the shadow of Sigmund Freud, whose totalising analysis attributed almost all of human conduct, and certainly all of humanity's social organisation, to the sexual instinct and its repression. Freud observed, not incorrectly, that individuals are powerfully interested in sex: it provides us, he said, 'with the prototype of all happiness'. He therefore thought it natural that a man 'should make genital eroticism the central part of his life'.[3]

But Freud did not therefore believe in a sexual free-for-all. He believed that without strict regulation society would become a permanent war for sex, with women reduced to chattels and the dominant males excluding other men, with socially catastrophic effects. So Freud explained civilisation as a means of repressing sexual freedom, and rationing and regulating sex on a moderately equal basis. This repression is necessary for peace, he argued, but it is bad for the soul, which wants more sex than it is allowed. To Freud, therefore, the price of peace is a neurotic, sexually frustrated population (albeit with the benefit of great art and creativity, which is the product of sexual energy needing an outlet).

Freud, then, was a reluctant conservative, recognising the need to contain sexual licence. His successors were not so inhibited. The 1960s generation agreed with him that 'genital eroticism' is the central part of life. But they did not agree with Freud's gloomy prediction of a Hobbesian sex-war in the absence of regulation. They did not agree that we need to repress eroticism to keep the peace nor – with Gerald Manley Hopkins – that keeping sex within proper bounds increases its pleasure and power. Who needs the 'sprung rhythm' of constrained sexuality when we can have 'all this juice and all this joy' without constraint, without limit?

We traditionally sought to contain sex in order to make it a bonding rather than a dissolving agent in society. We now do the opposite. Sex is presented as a means of self-definition and social freedom. As Carl Trueman has shown, twentieth-century theorists from William Reich to Herbert Marcuse and Simone de Beauvoir adapted Marx and Freud to sexualise the revolution, deliberately dismantling the cultural architecture that housed sex in the Western imagination in order to reshape society itself.[4] These thinkers regarded sexual freedom as a prelude to social liberation, a means of overthrowing a civilisation that was built not just on the repression of people's sexual urges but on the repression of people themselves.

Sex is properly a public act because it is the basis of human regeneration and the bonding agent of the couple relationships on which society depends. This, the sexual basis of the social order, used to be known and understood, and consequently not much mentioned. The healthy prudery that descended over sex in the Christian era reflected both the sacred quality of the subject and the confidence that it was under good management. Today we talk of almost nothing else.

Perversely, by privatising sex – abstracting it from its location in the foundations of society and reducing it to its basic function as a form of individual recreational pleasure, of no concern to any but the participants – we have caused it to saturate our culture. To get sex back where it belongs, behind closed doors, we need to restore its status as a public act done in private – rather than, as currently, a private act done (or all but done, and certainly explicitly celebrated) in public.

Thanks to advertising, and its offshoot the entertainment industry, our public streetscapes and our private

COVENANT

environments of screens and magazines are liberally deco-
rated with graphic sexual representations. And just beneath
the surface, officially out of view but as visible as a swimmer
in a swimming pool, is the world of sex on the internet. We
inhabit a pornworld, a public and private universe saturated
with the imagery of sex.

Pornography consists overwhelmingly of the humiliating
display of male power over girls and young women. No
more the 'Innocent mind and Mayday in girl and boy' of
Hopkins's poem; now it is the 'homogeneous script' of online
porn, the trillion films and images that portray a handful of
variations on the single theme of female degradation.[5] The
sexual revolution has come to this: a pornified adolescence
that gives boys the idea that they can do what they want
to girls.

The post-Freudian fantasy of sexual liberation was a
licence for male exploitation of women, surely as damaging
as the patriarchal system that preceded it. For the sexual
revolution did not just overthrow one gender role, the notion
of women as virtuous, vulnerable and requiring respect and
protection by men. It overthrew the other gender role too,
the notion of men as respectful, protective and trained to
restrain their desire for sex with strangers. We are realising
that this hasn't worked, and the disarray of sexual relations
is very naturally inducing a reaction.

The #MeToo movement arose in the wake of disclosures
of sexual harassment in Hollywood. Millions of women

across the West revealed that they also had been subject to violent, threatening, demeaning or simply inappropriate sexual attention by men. Subsequent waves of disclosure have exposed a horrible culture of sexual abuse at many schools and universities in Britain. The consequence is a growing sense that sex needs, once more, to be regulated.

But regulated how? The answer from the #MeToo movement is 'educate your sons'. This is surely right, although it rests on a thin diagnosis of the problem, and seems unlikely to work on its own. #MeToo reflects what Colin Gunton calls 'the greatness and the pathos' of liberalism: the attempt to make new rules in the absence of a common moral understanding.[6] Our sons inhabit the world we have made: the pornworld, and a moral scheme that has personal individual pleasure as its highest good.

I have suggested that the traditional conception of marriage recognised the difference and the complementarity of the sexes. It is instructive that even to mention sexual differences today, still less to try to particularise them, is politically dangerous. So detached is the new religion from the reality we all recognise that, rather like Queen Victoria, who reputedly denied the existence of lesbianism, it feels risky even to mention the interest many women have in childcare, or the aptitude many men have for war – notwithstanding the existence of many warlike women, and some men with an aptitude for childcare.

It is of course true that social and cultural expressions of maleness and femaleness (what we have recently come to call 'genders') are somewhat liquid, and indeed the ease with which one can travel back and forth between them has been a theme of art and literature in all times and places. Yet in our time in the West, this fruitful ambiguity has evolved rapidly into the more political idea that the terms 'male' and 'female' have no fixed meaning at all, but are purely constructed – and constructed, moreover, by and in the interests of a 'normative' that must be overthrown.

Paradoxically, however, the categories of gender are also honoured as deep-felt truths – the 'authentic self' is gendered, but not by biology (and certainly not by the patriarchy, in the form of a nurse or your parents deciding what you are at birth). Your gender is real, but it is your own discovery, your own creation.

'One is not born, but rather becomes, a woman,' wrote Simone de Beauvoir. 'The female is a woman insofar as she feels herself such.'[7] Here, in the words of Sartre's colleague and lover, is the fulfilment of existentialism. Here, at its purest, is the idea of the psychological self, whereby existence, mere corporeal reality, is superseded by essence, the 'realer' reality we construct for ourselves. Sex is existence – sex exists, materially – while gender is its essence, and thus of more significance than sex. The merely physical is surpassed by the more authentic, uncorporeal reality of what one 'feels' oneself to be.

'Transgender rights' involves the final and total disembodiment. It is an attempt to make unreal the most real thing there is. The psychological category of gender is preferred to the embodied reality of sex, and the body is then forced to adapt to the psyche, whether formally through law (with a 'Gender Recognition Certificate' stating you belong to the opposite sex to that of your biology) or practically through medication and surgery. The echo of the gnostic heresy, by which the material order is inherently evil and goodness only exists in the spiritual or psychic realm, is strong in trans ideology. It is the latest attempt to attribute evil to creation, to argue that wickedness exists not in the soul of human beings but in the material world around us.

This is all very wrong. Sex is the only real identity that a human being can have that is both immutable and meaningful. It is far deeper than the superficial identities of ethnicity or birthplace, far more important to us than the identities we get from our families or our country. Sex is the grand particular, the great binary fact that applies to all: you are one or the other, XX or XY, and if you are not (the vanishingly rare chromosomal disorder known as intersex), or if you feel you somehow 'are' the sex you are not, there is something sadly amiss.

You deserve compassion and help, not affirmation of the error – and certainly not the licence to behave as the opposite sex in all circumstances. For one effect of the transgender movement is that men with psychological disorders, confused in their sexuality and physicality, some of them patently dangerous, claim and frequently are given the right to enter spaces like changing rooms and bathrooms where women, in general physically weaker than men, are at their most vulnerable: naked, unprotected, extremely at risk.

THE HECATOMB

Transgenderism represents the penultimate destination of the Idea. The ultimate destination is obliteration. Hovering over the sex-cult is the angel of death.

Death is the externality of the Idea. When we live for ourselves, others must die. If we think we are good and creation is bad, we end up killing people. Instead of a pleasure dome, we make a hecatomb, a mass sacrifice of human life to the gods of our culture. This is the deathworks.[8]

The Western deathwish is evident in Western rates of childbirth and the campaign for euthanasia. Our fetish for sex abstracted from family life leads naturally to a reduction in baby-making. And the dissolution of families also leads, just as naturally, to the great disaster that is impending in the West: the deliberate killing of the old, the ill and the disabled.

The Idea abolishes sex the category. A very natural consequence is the decline of sex the activity. It is no real surprise that amid the kaleidoscope of images of beautiful people in unrealistic copulation, ordinary human beings are lonely, and not having much sex at all.[9] There is not much 'juice and joy' in the pornworld. As Freud predicted, we have a class of men – the 'incels', or involuntary celibates – who cannot get a partner from the small pool of women who satisfy the pornographic imagination. There is a correspondingly small pool of men who are able to earn the love of women. And so in the West we have an epidemic of singlehood, and of childlessness.

Other cultures, including our own in times gone by, made a virtue or even a fetish of fertility. In the modern West, it is seen as bad taste to relate sex to reproduction at all. 'Procreation' is a modern joke, said with a snigger, as if the continuation of the species and of the cultures which make it up – what Marcuse called 'the repressive order of procreative sexuality'[10] – is a risible concern. Sure enough, we are not procreating. In the UK, we face a grim milestone: by 2025, for the first time in history, more people will die each year than are born, and our population will only keep growing because of immigration.[11]

And so to the final fulfilment of the Idea, the natural culmination of the journey that began with the disembodiment and the disenchantment of sex. In the early twentieth century, progressive intellectuals became excited by the possibilities of using science to improve the species. Eugenics – the sterilisation of the undesirable or unsuccessful, and selective breeding for racial purity or social strength – was briefly a fashionable cause.

Eugenics lost its appeal to progressive opinion due to its enthusiastic application by the Nazis. But its twin, euthanasia, somehow escaped the censure of the fashionable world. In the post-war years, the campaign became about 'voluntary' euthanasia, and then more recently the more limited option of 'assisted suicide', by which a doctor, rather than personally killing their patient, prescribes the lethal drugs for the patient to eat, drink or inject themselves.

It is an apparent irony that, through the long centuries during which death was often drawn-out and painful, and the old, the disabled and the weak were genuinely a burden on families and communities, state-sanctioned euthanasia was never thought of; yet now that medicine is rapidly diminishing suffering at the end of life and we provide support, and indeed legal protection against discrimination and ill-treatment, to infirm and disabled people, our culture is clamouring for the right for doctors to administer lethal drugs to people whom they judge to be better off dead.

Of course, this is not how the Idea presents itself. The case for euthanasia rests not on one's vulnerability but on one's autonomy. Indeed, the term 'assisted suicide' conforms more neatly to the Idea than euthanasia. The Idea wants the fullest scope of action for the authentic self. And what greater expression of autonomy can there be but the power to determine the time and manner of your own death, to summon the assistance of the state to facilitate it and to execute the deed yourself? In the world of the Idea, the concern of government is not with society as a whole – whether evilly, as a means of strengthening the 'race', or benignly, as a means of protecting the most vulnerable. The concern of government is to facilitate individual choice.

Assisted suicide is presented as a necessity for only a handful of extreme and distressing cases. Yet the logic of the first step, the decision that some people should be killed with the help of the state, has an irresistible force. None of the limits and safeguards proposed by the campaigners (the period of your prognosis, for instance, or the nature of your condition – it is suggested that only people close to a natural death should be eligible for an artificial one) has any coherent basis. Why place a limit here rather than there? Why have a limit at all, if we're talking about a right? Each so-called safeguard would be naturally challenged in court by people denied a right now available to others, and Parliament, having conceded the principle, would find itself carried inevitably to further and further concessions in practice.

The Idea assumes that the individual is rightfully sovereign – 'autonomous' – over his or her own physical being. The purity, the absolutist quality of this belief, is apparent in its application to people *in extremis*, people who are in fact entirely dependent on the care of others. The advocates of autonomy suggest that the bigger the decision, the more independent you should be: that the more dwarfed the human being is by the immensity of the landscape, the more we should leave them alone; that in matters of life and death, the individual is singular, free and responsible. And so by force of logic we find ourselves pretending that the individual is infallible, capable of objective judgement in the most momentous decision it is possible to make while gravely ill and in anticipation (justified or not) of imminent terrible suffering.

The assumption of infallibility has a perverse corollary. The Idea admits the weakness and dependence of people at the end of life, and despises them for it. The individual of the Idea is heroic: strong, autonomous, capable of agency and of satisfaction in the pleasures of life. It follows that the individual who is not heroic – not strong and autonomous but disabled, distressed, incapable and incontinent – is better off dead. This is called 'dignity', as if dignity consists in keeping up the heroic image by keeping the sheets clean.

The apparent public support for assisted suicide flows partly from an understandable wish to minimise suffering. But I also think it flows, less creditably, from a submerged cultural prejudice against the old and disabled, and an unvoiced but widespread belief that frail or disabled lives are not worth living. The superficial popularity of the proposal reflects not only a society steeped in the doctrine of autonomy, which cannot imagine a counter-argument to the claim that 'people should be able to do what they want', but also a society that routinely neglects and even abuses the old and disabled.

In countries where euthanasia is legal, the majority of people who opt for it do so at least partly because they do not want to be a 'burden' on others; many are also lonely. Given a culture in which dependence, disability and even old age are despised, in which families are unable or unwilling to look after their old folk, it is little wonder that so many vulnerable people feel this way.

Euthanasia is the denial of relationship. Assisted suicide laws make no requirement for your relatives to be informed of your decision to die with the help of regulated medical professionals. One can see why not, perhaps – why should an estranged or abusive relative be allowed to intrude on this momentous decision? – but it is also extraordinary that doctors could deliberately bring about someone's death without their children or their partner knowing about it. This difficulty – whether or not your family has a right to know if you are getting government help to end your life – is indicative of the essential strangeness of assisted suicide, the discomfort it induces in people who think about its workings in real life.

Rather than the appearance of heroic invincibility, surely 'dignity' means being fully cared for, right to the end: it means an unstinting, unconditional attention to those who need the care of others, through life for those with disabilities, and for everyone through the whole time of their dying. Developments in the science of pain relief in recent years mean that no one has to die in physical agony; every year it becomes possible for more people to die well.

We now have the opportunity to create in the twenty-first century what in former times could only be dreamed of, though former times did their best at this: an arrangement for dying, with care at home or in a nearby place of peace and comfort, where pain is minimised and love abounds. The alternatives, a medicalised death alone in a hospital, or deliberately expedited by fatal drugs, we can leave with the horrors and dark fantasies of the twentieth century.

3

OIKISM

A VERY SHORT HISTORY OF THE WESTERN FAMILY

A better society is possible than the pornworld and the deathworks. We can avoid the collapse of systems, technological, ecological and social, that would trigger a civilisational disaster. But to avoid this fate, bluntly, we need to be better people. We need to wean ourselves off practices and beliefs that are harming us and our world, and commit with resolution to a better path. This path stretches forward to a good future, for it starts in the past.

Pre-industrial society was brutal, short and squalid, to be sure. But it was also enchanted, rich with the magic of the natural and supernatural worlds and structured around relationships that were not so much chosen as given. And it was embodied, with an economy centred on the home and the neighbourhood, sustained by the work of human hands. In this economy the resources that were used – people and the environment – were also the primary object of concern: ends as well as means.

Our culture seems to be searching for something like this. We want a life that is both embodied and enchanted: rooted, tactile, sweaty, but also lit by sacred fire. We want a life of function (to be useful and fully used) and of place (to identify with a piece of land and the people of it), and for these things to be both food for the body and food for the soul. I suggest this life can be realised by getting right a set of relationships and institutions: an Order. The first of these relationships and institutions is the family.

Oikos, the Ancient Greek word from which we derive 'economy', means 'household'. The *oikos* was the smallest viable unit of society, just strong and large enough to sustain itself as part of a network of other *oikoi*, generally kinship groups formed and reformed through marriage. For millennia, people maintained themselves materially through cooperative production within households, farming, manufacturing or serving in or close to the home, and trading with their neighbours. There was a job for everyone, male and female, young and old.

Industrialisation disrupted this model but did not immediately destroy it. The economy of the household, the work of many hands, close to home, a part of village life, was replaced by the economy of small 'nuclear' families dependent on a single wage earned in some remote occupation, in shop or office, factory or pit. Kinship groups survived, as David Brooks has argued, with interrelated urban households forming artificial villages to sustain life in the city.[1]

Yet the role of the home as a place of economic production steadily diminished. The idea grew – Dickens is perhaps most to blame – of the home as a place apart from the dirty, rough and increasingly masculine realities of economic life. Prosperity for a family came to be defined by the independence of the home, and of the female figure at its centre, from the grubby business of money-making.

The process was completed after World War II with the emergence of the suburban nuclear family of bourgeois legend and longing. The central role here was played by the woman as carer and consumer, responsible for home-making but not for economic production. And so *oikos* became *domus*: the place of sleeping, eating, watching TV and doing the laundry. Very naturally, this induced a reaction from women, who found their traditional economic roles, and the purposeful relationships that economic activity brought them, sacrificed to an ideal of domesticity that for many was profoundly unfulfilling. As Mary Harrington has pointed out, the post-war model is not, as conservatives today might imagine, the traditional way of things. The stay-at-home mother, confined to care and consumption, is an 'artefact of modernity', and not a sustainable or particularly happy one for most.[2]

The result was 'second-wave' feminism (after the first wave, which brought political and civil rights). Second-wave feminism was of course political in theory, in the spirit of the sexual revolution which sought deliberately to undo the social order, starting with the family and extending to wider society.[3] To most women, however, the appeal of women's liberation was not that it would destroy the status quo outside the home, but that it would allow them to join it.

The transformation of the Western economic model in the last quarter of the twentieth century accelerated the decline of the home. The industrial jobs that had sustained the single-earner household disappeared abroad, and in their places new jobs in the service economy opened up, for which women were at least as qualified as men: professional jobs in offices, and the work of caring for the growing number of old people and for the children of the other parents who went out to work.

As Miriam Cates MP has pointed out, for most women second-wave feminism and the service economy have not liberated them from domestic responsibilities but merely added financial ones, without the corollary of professional fulfilment. Most working women do not have a 'career'. They have a job, and often more than one, in a care home, in an office, in a supermarket. And they are still responsible for the housework, the children and the care of the elderly. It cannot feel much like liberation.[4]

The alterations in the economy since the 1980s have significantly lifted the material standard of living for most people in the UK. But there have been costs, too, most obviously in the time that is spent by adults in the home and the neighbourhood. No longer does marriage mean that between them the couple have to work less hard to earn enough money to achieve a decent quality of life. Wages relative to the costs of family life mean that both partners have to work long hours. The unromantic but effective incentive to settling down – the prospect of a better standard of living for less work – is gone for all but the asset-rich middle classes who can liquidate two small flats in the city and buy a big house in the suburbs, and even they can hardly reduce their hours. It is little wonder that the social incentives for marriage – the approbation of others, the sense of having joined the grown-ups in a large and privileged club – is gone, or going, too.

To summarise: in the last 250 years, English society has transitioned from a genuine 'oikonomy' in the pre-industrial period, where everyone, young and old, was actively involved in the creation of wealth for the household, to the industrial age, when, for a moment, and only in some places, and at some cost to the well-being of all parties, a small nuclear family could be sustained on the wages of a single (male) earner, to today's post-industrial economy, where a single wage doesn't nearly cover the family's costs, and parents work two or three jobs each and are still poor, and the home is just a depot for rest and refuelling where everyone is present only when everyone is asleep.

MOVING HOME

What is next? The household we need is a far cry from the mid-twentieth-century model of the nuclear family, with the husband working long hours far away and the wife looking after the children on her own. But nor is it the early twenty-first-century model, the feminist reaction to the earlier one: both husband and wife (or, increasingly, a single mother with no husband in sight) working long hours far away, and no one home, young children in all-day nurseries, older children left to their devices, and the elderly out of sight and mind in 'homes' where they are cared for by low-paid women who cannot afford to look after their own children or parents either.

Government has to generalise. Like any system, it will aim at some essential purpose, even if that purpose is not recognised or stated, even if the unstated purpose is (as it probably will be if it cannot be stated) the dissolution of the social arrangements that the system was originally designed to protect. The state cannot be neutral if is to be active. A government that involves itself in the lives of families must necessarily influence the shape those families take.

So it is that we have organised society not around the family, but around the figure of a single person living on their own. We have designed a social and fiscal system to help people live in midlife as if they had no partner, no parents and no children. The model is of course a response to reality, and self-reinforcing: as the cultural and economic forces of the Idea do their work of dissolution, as more children grow up without the support of a stable family life, as fewer people marry or sustain their marriages and more elderly people live alone, the state and the market adapt to cater for them.

And of course a policy of 'normative singleness' is easier both administratively and politically. Treating people as solitary units is simpler for the state – and apparently more liberal – than having regard for their relationships, their contingencies and dependencies. Policy aimed at individuals can pretend a neutrality about lifestyles and culture, and avoid the need to make invidious choices about how to help people in complicated personal circumstances; it simply arrives after the event, like the cleaner, or the ambulance, without judgement on the situation it is there to clear up.

It doesn't work, of course. Indeed the fallacy of a model designed around the young singleton is evident in the fact that young people suffer most from it. Our children have been set free and find themselves adrift: indebted, exploited, with reduced prospects of marriage, children, a home to own or a community to serve. Meanwhile, their older peers are reduced to solitude. Across the 'left-behind' towns of England, in the bedsits and cheap boarding houses that benefits can pay for, live the sad relicts of broken relationships, the photos of their lost children propped on windowsills: the products of an economy and a culture that disregards family life.

We need to do things differently. There is no simple formula that will work the magic we need, nor a general arrangement that will suit the circumstances of every family. So the objective should be to generalise well: to design public policy around a social model that works best for most people. Instead of structuring society around the life of a young singleton, we should organise for the conservative normative: for the married family with dependent children, with elderly parents and community obligations. We should do so not because everyone is like this or because this is the only good model of living, but because a society organised in this way will be better for everyone, including those who, by choice or circumstance, do not fit the normative pattern.

Man is a social animal, but society is a centrifuge: relationships, whether in families or communities, that are not held together by strong adhesive fall apart in time. The adhesive must be cultural and practical. We need to remind ourselves constantly, through ritual, respect and the telling of stories, why families matter. And we need to invest, through policy, in the material conditions of family life. We need to restore the economy to the *oikos*.

This economic shift is more than a tweak of some fiscal levers. We need as a society to make a profound alteration in the way we live. We cannot carry on as if the purpose of life is the restless quest. The alteration we need is the one that a single person, hitherto alone and self-focused, undergoes on falling in love, getting married and starting a family. We need to move from a one-bed flat to a family home. I call it 'oikism': an arrangement in which the general economy makes it as easy as possible to form and sustain a household.

SOMEWHERE, SOMETHING, SOMEONE

David Brooks laments that, after World War II, 'children were no longer raised to assume economic roles – they were raised so that at adolescence they could fly from the nest, become independent and seek partners of their own. They were raised not for embeddedness but for autonomy.'[5] He is right to lament the ill effects of this trend. Yet one cannot fail to see its appeal.

The traditional model of family life stifled the freedom of young people who had different dreams to those of their parents, and of women who wanted more from life than the drudgery of housework and childcare. The future we want is not a reversion to static trades and fixed gender roles. People's right to explore, to experiment and to make their own mix of the roles of parent, homemaker and breadwinner is essential to a dynamic economy, a fair society and a happy people.

Our challenge, then, is to restore the *oikos* without restoring the inequality of the sexes and the restricted opportunities for young people that the old model entailed. We need to put the home back at the centre of our politics, as the base of economic as well as purely domestic life: a place of value creation, not just 'downtime'; the subject and object, both source and purpose, of human effort – and to do so in a way that respects sexual equality and the right of every young person to make their own way in the world.

It has been well said (apparently first in the 1970s by the New Zealand politician Norman Kirk) that what a human being needs is 'somewhere to live, something to do, and someone to love'. These needs represent the objectives of a good social policy, applied to families no less than to individuals. To strengthen family life and restore the *oikos* we need good housing in the right places, jobs that sustain the home, and a decent system of care for children and dependent adults.

'Somewhere to live' – more than anything else, housing accounts for the chronic unaffordability of family life, and indeed for the paucity of wider social action in the community. All the available person-hours in a household are taken up in paid work, or in travelling to work. This reality is driven primarily by the cost of housing, which has risen from around a third of an average family's budget to a half today.

Demand for housing is growing partly because of population growth, mostly fuelled by immigration, and partly because of family breakdown: families that formerly required one home now require two. Meanwhile, the supply of housing is hopelessly constrained by the laws governing planning and development which hinder the building of attractive, well-made, affordable homes in the volumes and the locations where they are wanted.

The heart of the problem is our treatment of land as a normal asset, of the type that is created in response to demand, coupled with misguided rules about what can be built and where. The market for housing in the UK is a racket designed to benefit property speculators, or the 'volume housebuilders', as government respectfully calls them. These companies bet on the value of land, suppressing supply – the 'build-out' of new homes on the land they acquire – until local house prices reach a level that justifies the acquisition. The houses themselves are secondary assets, indeed hardly assets at all compared to the land they sit on; they are therefore frequently built with little love or skill, and less beauty.

The consequence of this model is steadily inflating asset values for those already on the property ladder, leaving ordinary families, and first-time buyers in particular, eternally behind. Rentiers – people who benefit from unearned income or capital appreciation – have a good reason to resist housebuilding that will lower the value of their asset, as well as a very natural aversion to the ugly, inappropriate developments that the speculators seek to impose on neighbourhoods if they can successfully game the planning system.

What to do? I said in the Introduction that the covenant of the land is civil society, the institutions that create out of a plot of earth a place for human beings. An essential feature of this covenant is the role of the community in the distribution of land and the homes that are built on it. Home ownership does not merely establish the *oikos*, putting capital into the foundations of the household economy. It establishes the household in a place, connecting the family to the neighbourhood in a way that brings the expectation, if not the absolute obligation, of active belonging and contribution to local society.

It is wrong that the process of creating homes is one in which local people are passive spectators, impotent and appalled as a new estate of ugly, overpriced 'executive units' is built on the edge of a village that is crying out for houses that local young people can afford, or as a block of one-bed apartments rises in a part of the city that really needs more family homes.

Demand for housing, driven by high immigration and family breakdown, need not grow forever, but it has grown and will grow for a time before those trends can be reversed. We have a chronic shortage of housing, to which the only answer is more housebuilding. The way to achieve this in a way that respects the rights of settled communities to the land they inhabit – which includes the wider geography beyond each household's own curtilage – is by empowering those communities to take responsibility for the housebuilding that their neighbourhood needs.

Since 2010 we have come some way towards meaningful neighbourhood planning, whereby local councillors and volunteers assess the supply and demand for housing in their area and agree on future development. This needs to be significantly streamlined and popularised, with far more public engagement via online systems as well as old-fashioned public meetings. But the essential need (and indeed what will drive public engagement) is for communities to derive the material benefits of new housing.

Across the country, in pockets large and small (mostly small), an old-new model of housing is growing, rooted in the tradition of property rights but recognising the covenantal nature of land. Community Land Trusts acquire land in the name of the community, build and then either sell or lease the homes at affordable prices to local people. The key to the model is that the cost of the land itself is taken out of the price of the house.

To expand this model – and to make the 'land discount' that they offer households affordable for the Trusts – we need a major programme of acquisition. Land Trusts should be helped to buy land at its current rather than its potential or speculative value, by being granted the lion's share of the 'planning gain' that landowners receive when planning permission is granted; publicly owned land that government has no need of should be transferred directly to them. Communities themselves would thereby have the means, the power and the responsibility to create the homes that local people need.

'Something to do' – people need fulfilling work that supports a family. The evolution of work is both exacerbating the threats of the present time – making family life harder than ever – and offering a route towards the better path we need. On the one hand, automation and globalisation have already abolished many manual roles, and are swiftly doing the same to clerical ones. Young people are climbing as fast as their talents, their family's assets and government policy can take them up the ladder of professional qualifications and employment to escape the rapacious robot that is devouring the rungs beneath them. Many are not climbing fast enough, and falling into the abyss of shiftwork and piecework: pay for occasional jobs and nothing in between. We face the dystopian prospect, already indeed partly realised, of two classes, one secure, healthy, busy and rich, the other poor, precarious and unwell.

And yet the evolving model of work in the twenty-first century heralds a far brighter alternative. The opportunity is before us to restore the rightful character of work: not a duty of drudgery undertaken miles from home at the behest of ever remoter bosses, but a vocation, performed close to home in fulfilment of a proper purpose. A vocation is a job of virtue, through which our natural and acquired skills are called forth and put to work for a purpose beyond ourselves, but which nevertheless satisfies us more than any hedonic pleasure can ('work is more fun than fun', as Noël Coward said).

What, in the age of tech, are the virtuous vocations, the roles that robots may be technically capable of but which nevertheless we rightly reserve for humans? They are in two categories: the jobs of creativity and the jobs of care.

It is not true to say that machines will only ever perform the routine functions of life, the jobs of harvesting, sorting and processing, while humans will always be needed for the 'higher' functions of design and innovation. Machines can do the creative things too: design airports, compose symphonies, invent treatments. Yet it is surely true to say that we want humans involved in the business of design and innovation. We want creativity because it makes humans fulfilled, as the practice of the virtues always does, and because it makes society prosperous, materially and culturally.

We need artisans and entrepreneurs, artists, inventors and innovators; we need builders and businesspeople, farmers and fishermen, all the ingenious and challenging trades that – whether they acknowledge their creativity or not – creatively improve and maintain the fabric of our lives. And we want creativity because it makes humans, and life on earth in general, safe. As well as learning the neutral skills of science, technology, engineering and maths, young people need an education in the moral foundations of society, so they can exercise the rightful authority that human beings have over the machine and, through artistic and intellectual creativity, over the production of meaning.

Care is an even more essential human virtue than creativity. Everyone knows from their own lives the foundational need for, and value of, human help when we are weak: at the start and end of life, and at moments of illness or trauma in between. The giving of this care may, possibly, be physically possible for some automaton of the near future, but it is unthinkable that we would ever want our children to be nursed by a machine, or a robot to hold our hand as we die. And all the time in between, weak or strong, we need the care of others, whether a doctor or a therapist, a teacher or a pastor, a youth worker or a personal trainer. We are made to look after one another, and through the giving and receiving of care we become what we most truly are: potent, dependent, related beings.

The jobs of creativity and care, the jobs that humans are best at and needed most for, should be deliberately supported through policy. We need more training places, funded by reallocating a good part of the university budget to these vocational skills; more professional qualifications and rewards; tax breaks and subsidies for businesses and workers in these sectors.

This shift, a leaning-in towards the work that the times require, will help more people into the well-paid jobs that can sustain a family on a single income, or at least make it possible for a family to live a decent life without the need for two adults to work sixty-hour weeks in distant and unsatisfying jobs just to pay the bills. The explicit intention of government should be a 'family wage', whereby the household is supported on the earnings of a single full-time or two part-time workers.

'Someone to love' – romance is not the business of the state. But what follows from romance is: the family, with all its attendant obligations. Larger homes and more local and more fulfilling work would significantly improve family life. And the final task to restore the *oikos* is to improve the systems that provide financial support for families directly, through the arrangements of tax and benefits and the subsidies available for the care of children, disabled adults and the elderly.

You get what you pay for, and we pay for singleness. Fiscal arrangements currently seem almost designed to undermine families, and to make the home as expensive and pointless as possible. The benefits system subsidises separation through the fact that a couple with two homes ('living apart together', as it is called in the system) receives more in total than they would if they lived together. Over the last decade, the introduction of Universal Credit has enabled a more accurate reflection of household finance and caring responsibilities in the benefits system. But the tax system takes no account of the taxpayer's family circumstances or responsibilities.

In 1990, Margaret Thatcher's government abolished the old system of household taxation, in which all the family's income was deemed the income of the husband, in favour of individual or 'personal' taxation. The intention was to simplify the system, to equalise the sexes and reflect the fact that, increasingly, both adults in a couple worked. But the effect has been to make the UK's tax system uniquely anti-family.

A single adult without children earning £50,000 a year will have disposable income putting him or her in the top 10 per cent of the income distribution. If he or she has children, the same adult, whether single or with a non-working partner, would be in the bottom half of the distribution. Some degree of relative wealth for an individual without dependants is understandable, but the disincentive to childbearing here is excessive. And this is something it is easy to change, if we were prepared, like other countries, to tax households rather than individuals, or at least recognise individuals' family responsibilities in their tax bill.

People with professional jobs are increasingly able to work from home. For middle-class people, the world is changing in a way that helps, allowing them to hire in care around their own increasing availability. The task is to extend this flexibility down the income scale, and give people who have less power over their working hours greater choice and control over the help they get to care for their dependants. At the moment, childcare subsidies are available to families who put their children into large professional nurseries for most of the day; that money is not available to support parents who want to care for their children themselves for some of the time, or to pay friends and family to do so.

The government also pays far more for 'residential' care for elderly people (i.e. when they live in an institution) than for 'domiciliary' care, which is given to them in their own home. This makes it economically unrealistic for many elderly people to remain in their own home or to live with their adult children. As with childcare, we need to shift the assumption of the system back towards families, entrusting them with the money and the responsibility to arrange the support their elderly relatives need.

Helping people find a home, a job to do and a way to care for those they love are the proper objects of a government that wants to strengthen the *oikos*, the economy of family life. Yet families also depend on structures and systems outside the *oikos*, to which we now turn.

4

A NEW SOCIAL COVENANT

DOMINION

In the preceding chapters, I outlined the catastrophic system risks that threaten us. I attributed these to 'the Idea', a religion of individual self-creation that unpicks the connecting fibres of society and ruins the person. Instead of the Idea we need the Order, an old-new arrangement of institutions and understandings, which between them create the conditions for virtue. And as the first step in building the Order I suggested we recover a politics of home and the household, what we might call 'oikism', to restore us to ourselves and to each other.

The Order starts with the *oikos* but does not end there. This final chapter explores some of the wider 'conditions of virtue' beyond the household – *par-oikos*, from which we derive 'parish' – and proposes a set of measures to nurture them. First I explore the conflict between the Idea and the Order in its most essential context, our treatment of nature and its dark shadow, technology. I then apply the principle of the social covenant to economic and social policy.

A restored Order, a new social covenant, must be founded on an understanding of the natural world and our place in it. This was obvious, intuitive, to our ancestors. Pagan culture attributed spiritual properties to the natural world and situated human beings firmly in it. The 'green man' of early modern iconography, his mouth and ears sprouting vines, was a creation of the Christian era, but his popularity lay in the echo of the pre-Christian order, when the woods were enchanted and people were not so different from dryads.

Christianity, by contrast, decided that rivers and trees were purely physical things, and that the life of the spirit was a monopoly of mankind. Yet while mankind was not 'of' nature, to the Christian he was still firmly 'in' it (and indeed material things were the channels of God's grace). The job of humans was to improve our condition by taking responsibility for the natural world. And so, while our environment was often hostile and we often abused our duty to treat it well, we knew ourselves to be at home there. As the most capable creature on Earth, we had 'dominion', the right of cultivation and the responsibility of stewardship.

The new faith, the doctrine of the Idea, builds on Christianity and distorts it. It retains the belief that mankind is not 'of' nature. But the detachment is complete. For it denies we are 'in' nature either, as fellow creatures with the other created things. Rather, we are above nature altogether. We are gods: not creatures but creators. Initially, we are gnostic creators whose sphere is the immaterial world where you can be whatever you want to be and 'truth' is whatever you decide it is. But we aspire to be creators of physical reality too, or at least engineers with the power to amend and edit reality in its foundations.

It is little wonder that as we assume the power to create moral truth, the condition of the real world – our health, and that of the planet we inhabit – steadily degrades. I suggested in the Introduction that self-worship progressively dismantles the social order on which our personal and social well-being relies. We know this because first it wrecks the natural order we depend upon. For in refusing to be subject to God we have not surrendered the authority that Jewish and Christian doctrine gave us over the material world. We have not returned to the pagan worship of wood and stone. Our power over nature remains, and indeed is amplified by the Idea. What was dominion – the responsibility to look after the Earth as a careful steward, and the opportunity to flourish by its cultivation – has become domination: the use of the Earth as if we owned the place, and cared nothing for it.

The effects are well-known. The world is suffering deforestation, drought, water pollution and a chronic loss of biodiversity on land and sea. In the British Isles, according to government figures quoted by Henry Dimbleby in his 2020 report *The National Food Strategy*, since 1930 we have lost half our ancient woodland, half our heathland and 97 per cent of our wildflower meadows. Most of our rivers are poisoned.

Zeus regretted making human beings, regretted they acquired fire. In the same spirit, David Attenborough has described our species as 'a plague on the Earth'.[1] And one possible reaction to the devastation we have wrought is to renounce our place in nature altogether: to let the plants and animals have back the Earth, and retreat ourselves to a pre-industrial or perhaps even pre-agricultural state of one-ness with nature. Yet here, too, is the Idea at work.

The anti-human impulse is another effort at abstraction, another refusal to be created in the form we have: a repudiation of our particular place in nature. For our place in nature is not the same as that of the insects and animals. The insects and animals truly have no sense of the value of the Earth; they genuinely are programmed to exploit it. The difference is simply that they have no power to dominate, and so their exploitation of the Earth is generally, collectively, benign. They 'coexist' with nature, albeit in a frequently brutal Darwinian struggle.

Not so us. We are programmed not to exploit but to cultivate. We could not coexist with nature if we tried – not unless we lost all the capabilities that make us human. We are as unable to renounce our superior capabilities as we are to survive without them, for our inferior ones – our ability to survive or endure in the wild, to feed and warm ourselves without technology – are laughably inadequate.

The problem is not our presence at the apex of nature but our practice there: our practice of domination not dominion. And we see the problem not only in nature but also in ourselves. Our treatment of the Earth as if it had no value is evident in the fact that we are ill. The revolution in farm productivity has been so successful that a quarter of all food grown in the UK is never eaten – little wonder, when the cost of food has fallen from a third of a household's budget in 1960 to less than a tenth today.[2]

But of course we pay in other ways. The miraculous gains in farm productivity that allowed the land to feed the swollen urban population in the twentieth century were achieved by farming practices that pollute the soil and water. Crowded livestock requires antimicrobial drugs to keep disease at bay, contributing to a crisis of antibiotic resistance in humans; we are creating perfect conditions for 'zoonotic', or species-jumping, diseases.

And other productivity gains are achieved beyond the farm gate, in the processing of food to make it cheaper and – to our unsophisticated tastebuds – more delicious. Our prehistoric appetites crave salt and sugar, and gladly the food producers oblige; it is indeed much cheaper to make food that is bad for us. The result is that a third of middle-aged adults are obese. The illnesses that obesity induces account for 40 per cent of the NHS's budget.[3]

For the sake of nature and our health we need a better food system, one that honours the land, the elemental thing out of which the covenants of civil society make communities for human beings. This system puts the health of the land at its heart, while remembering that the purpose of the land is the production of food for people. We will restore nature by restoring humankind's dominion over it. This requires direction and leadership but also sensitivity. For at the heart of the natural Order are farmers.

In Wiltshire, I see farmers urgently working to sustain the health of the soil and water in the face of bureaucratic and commercial pressures that push the other way. We need to break the grip of the large producers and retailers that bear down on quality, guard against foreign imports produced to worse standards than home-grown food, enable more local processing and give individual farmers more reason and opportunity to cooperate with each other in the processing of their produce and the protection of their common landscape.

The transformation of farming will bring back the insects and the flowers long suppressed by pesticides and made homeless by the destruction of hedges and verges. It will also bring about a return of people themselves to the land. Twentieth-century farming finished the job of the early-modern clearances, turning a once populated countryside into ranches for sheep and cattle and plains of monocultured crops. The new models I see emerging in Wiltshire can make busier landscapes, with more work for people to do – coppicing, digging, maintaining woods and ponds, and processing food in healthy ways on or near the farms where it is grown.

All this work of restoration, this undoing of modernity, is enabled and driven by technology. One example: the mixture of crops that is the natural way to cultivate the land is made possible on an industrial scale by artificial intelligence that can monitor the health of millions of plants across a landscape all at once. And in this way, 'symbiotic farming' (which as Dimbleby says 'dates right back to the Mesopotamians') is made productive enough for our huge modern populations. We can maintain the miracle of agricultural productivity achieved in the last two centuries without the destruction this miracle brought to the soil and water, and ultimately to our own health.

Technology is restoring an older, more sustainable Order. Another example: tech means we can get the energy we need to power the post-industrial economy from the natural resources – the wind, sea and sun, and the heat of the Earth itself – which, at far lower rates of productivity, powered the civilisations of old. Awesome alternatives, just as natural but inaccessible to our ancestors, are available, such as nuclear power or the huge promise of fusion.

To achieve a transition to these models we may need our own home-grown oil and gas for a while longer. But we can be confident that technology will unlock nature's generator just as it has unlocked nature's storehouse: energy, like good unprocessed food, could be cheap, abundant and home-grown, ensuring resilience in the face of global disruptions and freedom from the blackmail of suppliers. Our challenge and task is to make good and safe use of this immense resource, for tech brings danger.

Modernity offers vast benefits for humankind. We may be opening an age of abundance, long life and prosperity for all. Yet from genomics to artificial intelligence, from robotics to nanotechnology, we are blundering into a new world with only the faintest clue what it means for us. Indeed, the people who should be responsible for regulating these developments – we politicians and our shadows in the media – are almost universally clueless about them.

A tribe of humanities graduates run the country and the culture, with only a dim memory of GCSE science to guide us. In consequence, we are in thrall to a priestly class of professional scientists who, like the druids of old, reveal to the rulers the mysteries of the other world – or at least offer auguries which serve to excuse a decision. Government may be utterly bewildered, but at least it can 'follow the science', as in the old days it heeded the flight of birds or the entrails of a chicken. We are currently following the science into captivity.

The immediate risk is national. The hegemony of the US and particularly China, and of vast American and Chinese

corporations in the new industries of data, digital, micropro-
cessing and data storage, threatens a terrible new dependence. If we are not careful we will awake (perhaps we have
already awoken) to find ourselves citizens of some bleak new
empire of tech, headquartered in California, in Shenzhen or
in cyberspace.

The more profound risk is not to the UK or to the West
but to humanity itself. The conflict between environmental
dominion and domination is the archetype of the battle for
tech in the modern era. As with the environment, there are
two visions of how human beings relate to the created order.
Dominion involves the use of art and science to reflect the
world as it is and to improve it. Domination is the practice
of self-assertion and the development of technology for
exploitation.

The battle becomes acutely significant in our age, as we
finally gain the power to make machines in the image of
ourselves. But what image is that? Will the robots have
the qualities of a related being, rooted in society and in
nature and subject to a common conception of the good?
Or will the machines resemble human beings not in their
dependency and virtue but in their independence and
power: self-created, unconnected and authentic; autonomous, rootless, relation-less; free of others, free from the
ideas of good and evil, programmed only to dominate
and exploit? Will the machines belong to the Order, or
to the Idea?

Our future under the latter dispensation is not likely to be good. Iain McGilchrist tells the story of a local king, the Master, who sees his kingdom grow and so appoints a vizier or 'Emissary' to administer the new territories on his behalf. The Emissary has the skills for the job: he is tireless, dispassionate, ordered and efficient. In time, however, the Emissary becomes too powerful: he concludes he is the effective and therefore the rightful king, and so he overthrows the Master and rules in his place. But the Emissary has nothing to say to the human heart, no sense of the relationships between people or their obligations to past and future. In my scheme, he rules through contracts not covenants, and embodies the Idea not the Order. So in due course and naturally, the kingdom falls apart.[4]

McGilchrist's book is about the rightful supremacy of the right hemisphere of the brain over the left hemisphere, of feeling, relationship, art and moral sentiment over the functions of analysing, sorting and ordering. The two sides of the brain need each other – and indeed each fulfils aspects of the other's functions – but the right side should rule the left. So it is with human beings: we are the rightful Master, and tech is our Emissary. But as things stand, the Emissary is on the point of taking over.

How do we rein in tech before it is too late? There is no single, indeed, technical answer to this challenge. The main thing is to recognise the need for a proper ethical framework for technology and to organise the analysis and the conversations that will assemble it. We need to build systems that scrutinise and where necessary challenge or even prohibit technologies that threaten social safety and well-being.

This power of prohibition will be a limited one, of course. We should be enthusiasts for the promise of tech and ambitious in particular for the UK tech sector, not least because if the UK, and countries with similar values, do not take the lead in technological innovation, other countries, with different values and a weaker ethical framework, will gladly do so.

The starting point is to remember who is boss. We need an attitude of unabashed human chauvinism, for the natural world's sake and our own. This is especially necessary as the possibilities of artificial intelligence unfold, and particularly the imminent reality of artificial general intelligence, of machines that are not simply programmed for a particular function but are capable of turning their robot hands to anything, and indeed of deciding what to do for themselves.

This dark glory is almost upon us. It could turn out to be catastrophic – not least for democracy, which will find itself overseeing less and less as the technium assumes responsibility for more and more. But it could equally turn out well, a big event but not a bad one. The vital thing, as Professor Stuart Russell said in his 2021 Reith Lectures, is to prevent the complete autonomy of machines by building into AI as a fundamental feature a commitment to serve the preferences and interests of mankind, as an adaptive and deferential servant.

The only safe foundation for the age of tech is human virtue. This, not 'science', 'progress' or 'reason', is the proper basis for our engagement with the world and for our use of the world's powers to further the ends we think are good. To ensure a virtuous relationship with tech we need to make sure it honours the associations that make us virtuous ourselves.

Does a given technology serve or harm family life, the neighbourhood or the nation? In the service of the nation we need to assert 'tech sovereignty': resilience against hostile penetration of our critical national infrastructure, and the development of a genuinely UK-based tech sector (rather than just performing an R&D function for other countries and mega-corps).

Tech can serve communities and families, but let us start with an extreme suspicion of its intentions, not least because of its ability to empower agencies – including the agencies of the state – which need their power curtailed. Importantly, tech sovereignty must not aggrandise government at the expense of citizens. We should explore options for community data ownership – the right of the neighbourhoods and groups that government and the tech firms analyse to have some say in the exploitation of the information that is extracted from them – and develop a form of digital *habeas corpus* that protects the rights of individuals to their own data.

Tech can help strengthen families and communities; the WhatsApp era has seen a great enhancement of communications among neighbours and extended families. Yet good relationships within households and neighbourhoods are sustained face to face, and ease of communication or access to information does not always make us happier and healthier – especially when what passes for information is really trivia, misinformation and all the other things our basic instincts give rapt attention to when the chance is offered. In this light, an urgent conversation is now underway about the role of social media, and the capabilities of smartphones in particular, in childhood and adolescence. It is not too late to close the stopper on this particular evil genie.

PLACE

I have argued that we need to restore our dominion over and our responsibility towards the land, and also to restore a measure of national sovereignty over the critical industries of food, energy and technology. That is the framework for a better economic model. Put simply, we need to reorient our economy towards the home and the community, the *oikos* and the *par-oikos*. We need to make families and communities as much the object of economic policy and political concern as they are the concern of people themselves.

Where and how did the economy, and our economic discussions, become so detached from these ordinary and essential things? The answer is partly historical, of course. Land enclosure and then industrialisation brought millions of people from settled rural neighbourhoods to the new urban centres. Nineteenth-century writers – Marx and his followers, but also Tories like Carlyle and Disraeli – noted (and the Tories lamented) the dislocation of social and economic life that this move wrought. But as David Brooks, cited previously, observed, it was possible to maintain family and community life in the city by means of large kinship networks and the artificial – covenantal – associations that urban life made possible and necessary: the credit unions, friendly societies and trade unions which emerged to give institutional life and social protection to the new society of the industrial age.

The real dislocation arguably came later, with the process of deindustrialisation that began once the UK had exported its manufacturing techniques to the rest of the world. The assumption of the free-market economists who oversaw deindustrialisation was that capital and labour, having found each other spontaneously to create the great urban centres in the nineteenth century, would equally spontaneously redistribute themselves in an age of industrial decline. As the factories closed, capital would flow in to take advantage of cheap land and labour, and unwanted workers would flow away to new opportunities elsewhere.

Neither happened, or not enough. It turns out that capital needs more than derelict buildings and wrongly skilled people to invest in. And it turns out that places are sticky: that people would rather stay with what they know, connected to the places and people they love, than 'get on their bikes', as Norman Tebbit said, for a precarious life in a distant city. The people who got on their bikes – or on planes, into the backs of lorries and into rubber dinghies to cross the Channel – were the ambitious and the desperate from the developing world.

Cheap foreign labour has been good for GDP, and for employers, and for consumers with disposable income for whom the services that enhance the experience of life – cleaning and gardening, carwashing and nail polishing – are more affordable than before. It has also brought into the necessary services like childcare, elder care and the food business an army of industrious, conscientious workers content with low wages.

Yet immigration, particularly on the scale we have had in the past twenty years – adding seven million people to the population of the country between 2000 and 2020 – has been bad for British workers (as GDP per head is not improved but reduced by the import of low-wage workers), bad for our economy in general (as the supply of cheap labour does away with the need to invest in the underlying factors of growth, technological innovation and investment in the skills and well-being of people) and bad for many British places, which have changed quickly and irrevocably.

If the free movement of labour has both obscured and exacerbated the decline of local communities, the role of capital has compounded the problem. According to the governing doctrine, the investment of public funds, if necessary at all, should be 'spatially blind', i.e. not concerned about place, but just aimed at whatever the spreadsheets say will generate the biggest return on investment. The calculation of return on investment, of course, naturally favours the deployment of capital in 'high-value' places, like London and the South East, or Oxford and Cambridge.

Thus, most egregiously, Treasury rules stipulate that the public housebuilding budget must favour building new homes in areas of high house prices, rather than on regenerating down-at-heel places to make them more attractive to mobile businesses and workers. So rather than a genuinely neutral policy reflecting the wishes of the public – let alone a policy reflecting the obligation to support the people and places affected by deindustrialisation – successive governments have 'blindly' reinforced the inequality that existed already.

Meanwhile, private capital has not flowed into the former industrial towns, but has continued to seek its returns in London and the South East, especially since the financial crisis of 2008. The capital created and released into the economy by low interest rates and the alchemy known as quantitative easing did not seek new investment opportunities in the North and Midlands, but found easy returns in rapidly inflating assets – mainly housing – in the South East. The price of keeping the financial system afloat was greater asset inequality than ever – and greater debt.

The two classes that emerged from deindustrialisation, free movement, 'spatially blind' public investment and quantitative easing were not the industrialists and workers of Marx's scheme. In London and the South East, and some urban centres further afield, there was development of the finance economy and its satellite specialisms, notably accounting and legal services but also latterly the new industries of advertising and consulting. A creative sector grew, too, to cater to both elite and popular tastes. But beyond these new enclosures the rest of the country struggled for employment and purpose.

Spatial inequality reflects the extreme variance in productivity – the ability to create economic value – between the two economies we have created. The UK has some super-productive firms creating innovative products, including in advanced manufacturing, as well as brilliant services. But most businesses make up the 'long tail' with a productivity equivalent to that of Eastern Europe. We can boast of what Dan Wang calls the 'sounding-clever industries' like finance, media and the law, in which the UK undoubtedly excels.[5] But while these industries enhance our brand among global trend-setters, and make London one of the world's great destinations for mobile talent, they create far fewer jobs and little wealth compared to the businesses – most of them now abroad – that actually make the things that people need.

These businesses may take some design and innovation from the UK, but our real role in the modern global economy today is to provide them with finance in the City, and then to provide customers for them in the City's hinterland, namely the rest of the UK.

Our chronic spatial inequality is built on our chronic trade deficit. Because the City attracts foreign capital for the services it provides, the pound is kept artificially strong, increasing the purchasing power of British consumers by making imports cheaper. The losers are British producers, who struggle to compete with foreign firms in both the domestic and the export markets, when they have to pay for their inputs (labour and materials) with expensive sterling.

What would a covenantal economy look like? In the previous chapter I outlined policy for the *oikos* – a focus on family-sized houses, on jobs that suit family life, and on systems of care for children and dependent adults that strengthen families. Policy for the *par-oikos*, the community beyond the household, should be built on the fact that an economy exists in a place, not the abstractions of 'the City', or 'globalisation', or 'cyberspace'. These phenomena – the finance industry, the reality of foreign competition and markets, the technologies that enable market exchange – are or should be subsidiary to the actual production of value that goes on in the streets, the industrial estates and the fields near where people live.

An old-new consensus is emerging to challenge the assumptions of economists that places are simply aggregations of commercial activity, the communal version of the fiction *Homo economicus*. The identity of a place, its heritage, environment and culture, matters as much as its transport links and business facilities. A place needs a sense of itself to hold its bright young people, and to attract others to settle there. New industries build on the foundations of old ones, whose traces can still be seen. Great Grimsby was once Britain's, indeed Europe's, leading fishing port. It is reinventing itself as a centre of offshore wind, while the historic docks, formerly a polyglot entrepôt, are transforming into a centre of the creative industries, both proudly local and boldly global.

Villages and market towns left behind by industrialisation, long denuded of labour and with the professional middle class relocated to big offices in the cities – places like Devizes or Marlborough in my constituency, which were major regional commercial and civic centres in the Middle Ages and into the industrial era, when they were eclipsed by Swindon, the railway town – are becoming viable once again: places of enterprise in both the old and the modern economy. The internet is rejuvenating local retail and services, helping revive traditional businesses – not least food production and processing – and attracting to the countryside the high-tech industries which are increasingly to be found in old farm buildings and small industrial estates on the edges of our towns.

To help the local economy grow we need a planning regime that supports the opening and expansion of premises, and a tax regime that rewards productive local businesses and, crucially, investment in productivity-enhancing capital improvements and the skills of local people. To this end, the UK badly needs a local finance sector to complement the global one based in London – like Germany's, where a network of regional banks provide patient capital to both established and start-up businesses to help them innovate and grow.

The goal is a revival of British manufacturing. Here is the real opportunity for a revolution in our productivity and a correction of our trade imbalance. Rather than an economy built on cheap credit, cheap foreign labour and cheap foreign goods – an economy whose purpose and motive force is consumption for its own sake – we need an economy of production, where the purpose of a business is to make something valuable in itself.

A covenantal economy is one in which the interests of the players – capital, labour, consumer, and the wider community and environment affected by the business – are aligned. This alignment does not preclude negotiation or competition, or even conflict between these players, and the resolution of these conflicts may require different mechanisms. The interests of producers and consumers can only be reconciled through a genuinely competitive market where the price mechanism generates a deal that suits both parties.

Similarly, bosses and workers need a free market, with a choice of places to take their capital or their labour in order to get a fair price for a day's work; they also need mechanisms outside the market, including trade unions, to help manage their relations. The interests of wider stakeholders may need political regulation to ensure that the 'externalities' of economic activity, such as the effects on the local soil and air, are properly reflected in the costs and prices of the business.

These are the proper systems of the covenant, the means of making the 'artificial brotherhood' that is necessary for the common life of many people. When they work well – when markets, labour relations and the management of externalities are all properly regulated – the interests of all align. A good economy is not one of antipathy, a zero-sum game where the object of the exercise is for each player to extract as much value as possible from others. In a good economy, the players produce value together, apportioning cost, risk and reward appropriately to the contribution, capacity and needs of each.

This holds true at any scale, including the global, where grand alliances of finance, raw materials, production, marketing and distribution span continents – but it works best and most necessarily at a local level. Here the pursuit of profit is essential, for the profit of a company is the livelihood of the individual or family whose time and capital are all the assets the company has. But here also profit is just one of a set of motivations that includes the pleasure of the work, the status and satisfaction it brings, and the contribution it makes to the local community or the world at large.

A truly free market, as every genuine apostle of the creed since Adam Smith has argued, depends on the proper moral orientation of businesspeople. As Professor Colin Mayer has shown, the modern company was awarded privileges in law and the tax system because it has a wider social value than the enrichment of its investors.[6] This was understood historically, but in the age of capital it required explicit iteration. Properly speaking, a business is covenantal, belonging to the civil society of a place: it is part of the associational life that makes a human neighbourhood out of mere geography.

Restoring this principle in our time is a job not just for government but for culture as a whole. Indeed, the trend of business in this direction – with the strong recent focus on 'purpose' – is positive, although it is frequently confused with the fashion for 'Equity, Diversity and Inclusion', and other corruptions flowing from the Idea. We need conservatives to seize the 'purpose' agenda. One way would be to add to the corporate forms or 'company types' that businesses can adopt, to include one that recognises a wider set of obligations than returning profit to their owners.

If the culture, the tax system and the wider system of regulation helped businesses focus not just on short-term 'shareholder value' but on their reason for existing – to do or make something that is valuable in itself and which people need or want – we could more closely realise the conservative vision of a low-tax, light-regulation economy.

For as Burke said, 'a controlling power upon will and appetite be placed somewhere; and the less of it there is within, the more there must be without'.[7] In the absence of an inner purpose we have compliance – the thickets of legal and regulatory oversight that chokes enterprise. A more purposeful commercial sector would enable us to cut away these thickets and become a more genuinely entrepreneurial economy.

CIVIL SOCIETY

The post-war welfare state was built on the foundations, and with something of the principles, of the Order. The great programme of state funding in healthcare, education and welfare was a response to the extremity of distress suffered by working people in the 1930s as the Industrial Revolution faltered. Thus the 1945 model had been long in the planning, and reflected existing institutions.[8] The welfare state in its beginnings had a high degree of institutional pluralism, of independence and discretion for front-line professionals, and an expectation of personal, family and community responsibility.

The role of faith groups and other independently governed schools in education was preserved; family doctors remained self-employed rather than state employees; welfare was still organised around the contributory principle of national insurance; and there was no such thing as 'social care', for it was expected that families and, failing that, local charitable organisations would look after people recovering from ill health or gradually declining towards death.

The early welfare state retained covenantal relationships at its heart, with some idea that the virtues were as necessary to its success as state funding and regulation. The story of the public sector since 1945 is the story of the supplanting of the Order by the Idea: of the steady dissolution of covenantal relationships in favour of contractarian ones, and overall, of the loss of virtue as the governing ethic of public institutions in favour of the more passive ethics of equality, efficiency and service. The result has been less equality in practice, less efficiency and poorer service.

The process got underway properly in the 1960s, with the aspiration for 'universal, comprehensive' coverage: all the needs of all the people, to be met by the state. The plan was not just that everyone would have access to the services they needed, but that these services would be delivered by the government, in the same way, in the same institutions, for everyone. A great new programme of hospital building was undertaken, standardising healthcare and shifting the focus from the organic system of general practice and community hospitals to large acute or 'general' hospitals.

The comprehensive school was born: all the children of the neighbourhood were collected in a single modern building and given the same education, regardless of differences in their abilities or interests. And in welfare, the social doctrine of the day, which ascribed human circumstances to structural forces beyond individual control, led progressively to a model of unemployment support very different from the temporary assistance, earned through contributions made during the years of work, of the National Insurance system: people became entitled to permanent support, limited only by national budgets.

The doctrine of universalism and the creation of great new state institutions led, in fairly short order, to disappointment. As the economic policy of the 1960s and 1970s spluttered into a stall, so we saw widespread failure in the public sector. This was because universalism represented in practice a great transfer of power from the beneficiaries or users of public services to the people who organised and delivered them: the managers in the bureaucracy of local government and the health service, and to the trades unions representing their staff (front-line staff themselves – teachers and doctors – were not much empowered by the changes). The result was not just a worse service. 'Producer capture' also established a set of ideas and practices deriving directly from the neo-Marxist ideas prevalent in the intellectual atmosphere of the time.

The materialist doctrine of the economy was reflected inversely in cultural and economic theory, where, as we have seen, the heirs of Marx and Freud adopted a gnostic view of individuals, capable of discovering or creating their own essence in defiance of apparent reality, certainly in defiance of any inherited norms or understandings. The notion of the person as inherently pure and good, and only harmed or harming others because of unfair structures created by the powers that be, found fertile soil in the public sector.

No longer was it thought necessary to ground children in the essentials – especially the rules of grammar which regulate our common language and so enable our common existence – for these essentials and their rules were the tools of the regime that must be overthrown. The idea of education as effecting the transmission of society's evolving knowledge and culture from generation to generation gave way to the attempt to inspire young people with the imaginings of John Lennon ('no heaven... no countries... no possessions'); not to induct them into the world they were inheriting, but to liberate them into a world they had the opportunity and the necessity to make for themselves.

The structures of the NHS – centralised, hospital-led, with the patient having neither responsibility for their own health nor choice over their care – has exacerbated the general trend towards a medical model of human health. The word 'patient' has of course long since evolved from the notion of one enduring suffering to one simply undergoing treatment provided by others, and of course this development is a marvellous achievement.

But if we were to make a new noun from an adjective, we might call the recipient of modern healthcare a 'passive'. And a mechanical passive, indeed: modern medicine treats the body as a machine to be 'fixed', when it breaks down, by expert professionals, with the predominant fix being a pill or injection from the pharmacopoeia. A quarter of the adult population is on antidepressants. This pharmacopoeia is the property of vast commercial interests deriving a handsome profit from the client of their dreams: the comprehensive, universal NHS, committed to treating everyone with everything they need, including those dependent on addictive and expensive drugs, and to paying for it with public money, on behalf of a public who constantly call for more spending on the NHS.

Since the early 1990s, governments have sought to address these problems. In some respects, particularly in education and welfare since 2010, we have seen real improvements as proper teaching of the basics was enforced, parents were empowered with greater choice over schools, and the benefits system adapted to support families and make work pay. Major challenges remain in these areas, however. And in others, the reforms have not helped at all but arguably made things worse.

'New Public Management', which began under John Major before 1997 and then accelerated under Tony Blair, was the attempt to introduce greater efficiency, value for money and choice for 'users' (or, as they increasingly and tellingly came to be called, 'consumers' or 'customers'), through quasi-market disciplines such as the 'purchaser-provider split', unit costs, targets and league tables. At the same time, the 'real' market was given a steadily greater role in the provision of public services.

This might have meant a revival of the Order, a return to a more plural arrangement of care provided by a large range of independent charities and companies competing for business in a way that empowers patients and their representatives who commission local services. But in fact it meant that a small number of commercial operators, owned by shareholders or private equity firms based in, and extracting profit to, the US and elsewhere, has moved into the British health and social care 'market', including the running of children's homes and old people's homes. Thus the most human, the most sensitive of services, the provision of homes to the vulnerable young and old, are the subjects of contracts between the public sector and Wall Street.

There is a better way than this. We need to restore, and renew for our times, a covenantal model of the public services. This model would reflect the essential features of the Order, namely human virtue – the 'excellences of the species' by which we fulfil our responsibilities to other people and become our best selves – and the associational life, the institutions that create the conditions for virtue to be nurtured and practised. The better way is built on the twin principles of personal responsibility and civil society.

The reform programme we need starts with the dismantling of the priesthood which governs the thinking and
management of the public sector. The acute paradox that
cripples the system, ever-increasing budgets and permanent
shortages on the front line, can be resolved by stripping away
the hierarchies of impervious bureaucracy to make public
services that are more local, more human, and more cost-
effective. Services should be organised around communities
with a recognised identity, with the names of real places and
the means for local people to hold them to account.

We have looked at the means of strengthening family life,
which is the best foundation for the production of responsible citizens. The role of schools is to augment the work of
the family, providing inputs that most families would struggle to organise themselves: education in the pedagogic sense,
and also socialisation in the virtues and expectations of life
outside the home. Some families can organise this, and it is
worth stating that the basis of the universal education offer
is the now somewhat niche and eccentric model known as
home schooling.

This model, and the right, still just preserved in law, of
any parent to opt for it if they choose, reflects the fact that
the education of a child is properly the responsibility of
its parents. This does not mean that parents are allowed to
dictate what, if anything, their children should do all day.
'Education' is a meaningful thing, and the associations above
the family, i.e. the neighbourhood and the nation, rightly

insist that all children are educated according to some collective sense of what it entails.

A covenantal education system should see schools as the point of confluence of all these associations, where all their interests and values meet, and are modified and aligned. The basics of education, the pedagogy of what is taught and how – most essentially in the basics of grammar on which all human communication relies – needs to be mandated by government acting on behalf of the nation as a whole. The school gets its flavour from the local community, which may include a strong dose of religion, so long as the dose includes a respect for individual rights and universal norms. But the most important player of all is the family, who, though obliged to ensure their child is educated according to the expectations of the country, need the most essential power: to choose the place and people who will provide the education.

The education system we have has the right basic structures: parental rights and responsibilities; community ownership of many schools, whether accountable to the local council, a church or religious body, a charitable educational trust or a board of parent governors; and state funding and overall regulation. The challenge is to ensure that each part of the arrangement lives up to its responsibilities. We need all parents to be as engaged and responsible as many, though not all, already are; the governing bodies of schools, the incarnation of the local community, to insist on the best standards and on good values; and the state not only to properly fund but to properly regulate the system as a whole. The impetus to all this is cultural: a revival of an understanding of the virtues and their place at the root of a good society.

A school should reflect the values of the family, the neighbourhood and the nation, not those of activists trying to change the basis of society. This is why it is so wrong that children are taught alternative sexual ethics, often without their parents knowing what is happening. We need very deliberately to drive the transgressive ideology out of schools by top-down action to ensure the curriculum reflects the customary values of the country; by the empowerment and accountability of governing bodies to take responsibility for the non-curricular activity that the state cannot regulate; and by ensuring choice and influence for parents. The result would be no 'drag-queen story time'; no noticeboards plastered with menus of possible gender expressions and hectoring injunctions to normalise the strange; no validation of precocious sexuality in children, nor pornography masquerading as 'relationships and sex education'; and no 'critical race theory' in the history and literature curriculum.

If the structures of education, though not all its content, are sound, the structures of health and welfare are not. Their foundations are the Victorian working-class communities who organised mutual insurance programmes to protect themselves against the disasters of illness or unemployment. The buildings we have now, our modern systems of health and welfare, are totally different. But in these old foundations we can find the outlines of the combined system we need to build.

We need health and welfare to be local, and we need individual citizens to be responsible, invested and empowered. I have suggested that the subsidies offered for childcare and adult social care should augment, not replace or sideline, the support that families give to their dependants. Benefits in general should reflect the circumstances of a household, rather than simply those of the individual – as they partly do, thanks to the recently introduced system of Universal Credit. But we could go further, especially in the support we offer new parents, or someone whose parent or adult child is suddenly disabled or dependent.

The 'benefit' here is wrongly named: what is being paid for is the production of value, namely the care of someone who needs it, and by the person best placed to give it. The model for organising this payment should be founded on the responsibility that people have to their families; the exercise of this responsibility should generate additional support by wider society.

Paid leave to care for your family should be funded through insurance. We need a system that requires people to make a contribution to a fund that they will draw upon when the usual or unexpected events of life occur, like a change of career or the demands of a family. Government pays the premiums, in whole or part, according to need.

Insurance could pay for healthcare and social care too, as of course it already does for millions in the private market. In Germany, Japan and elsewhere everyone is insured, by law. The insurers are, like the mutual and friendly societies of Victorian England, mostly local or rooted in a particular sector or profession.

Thus the purposes of the different players in the system are aligned. Insurance is contributory, communal, long-term, and it demands responsibility of the individual participants as well as of his or her community. It allows a better model of healthcare and welfare to develop than the mechanical paradigm of 'fixing' broken people. An example already in use in places is 'social prescribing', by which GPs offer patients with non-acute physical or mental health conditions alternatives to pills, such as a gardening group or a walking club.

For often what someone needs, more than medication, is time spent off the sofa, ideally outdoors, ideally working up a sweat, in the company of others, and making themselves useful. Through social prescribing, the NHS is encouraged artificially to simulate a functioning community, where we do not get depressed or obese because there is so much for us to do. Naturally, the model works better in some places than in others, according to the local culture and leadership among GPs and the independent organisations providing the activity. But in some places it works spectacularly well.[9]

The success of social prescribing reminds us that civil society, the medley of local institutions formed for a variety of civic and social purposes, is the covenant that makes a neighbourhood. Nor are civil society organisations simply peripheral or nice to have. The public services responsible for health and welfare themselves began life as independent local institutions, created by communities to meet communal needs.

Even the agencies that deliver the coercive functions of the state, executing the decisions of the courts with respect to the detention of criminals and the care of children at risk of abuse or neglect, need to be 'civil' in their operations. These statutory responsibilities are only successfully fulfilled when the agencies of society – charities, families, communities in a multitude of different forms – play their part too, humanising the prison or the children's home, helping broken relationships heal and new ones form, and ensuring as far as possible that the individual who has been the ward of the state can in future be a good member of society.

Civil society calls forth virtue in its members, both those in need of help or correction and those providing it, who may change positions from one month to the next. And the giving of help to others is crucial. Among the worst features of the times is the crisis in purpose in men and women.

We have been taught that we have nothing to live for beyond ourselves, nothing that justifies the loss of a moment's repose or pleasure except the tedious necessity of generating wealth for our own use. We have commissioned government to do the difficult business of looking after our neighbours in need, thereby obviating our greatest and most natural purpose, the fulfilment of our duty of care to others.

And so it is that the business of community life – working with young people or the elderly, maintaining and repairing the physical infrastructure of the neighbourhood, restoring the green spaces and the rivers, running public events, making public art and preserving the local culture, and all the detailed committee work of local leadership and decision-making – is outsourced to contractors; or done by a handful of harassed and stressed-out volunteers; or simply not done at all.

The extreme stress felt by front-line professionals in the public services is an effect of their caseload, the shameful ratios of support under the current model: thirty children to one teacher; one or two hundred prisoners to one prison officer; a dozen elderly or disabled people to one care worker. As well as getting more money to the front line of these services, we need more people in them. We should be flooding the system with personnel, paid, unpaid or this way earning their benefits.

These workers and volunteers could drastically improve the quality of services we provide, relieving the pressure on specialist professionals who are currently overwhelmed by their caseloads. Already, but not nearly enough, volunteers contribute significantly to the life of hospitals and care homes, spending time with patients that doctors and nurses cannot spare. In schools, volunteers could play a transformative role helping individual children with their studies, or leading activities (such as sports) that the school cannot afford to organise. Prisons, probation and youth offending services could likewise benefit from the right help, by people trained and managed as necessary but qualified most of all in common sense, duty and compassion – qualified in the virtues.

To realise the abundance of 'human resources' that lies latent in society, and put it to use for the benefit of both the public services and the people who, being useful, would themselves find purpose and greater wellness through the work, of course requires significant changes to our economic model. I outlined above the necessary ambition we need in the world of work, to achieve a 'family wage' that can support a household on the earnings of one full-time or two part-time adults.

The objective here is to create time that can be put to a better purpose than commuting to a distant job for low pay and little satisfaction. The benefits system we need – insurance-based, managed through local or sector-specific mutuals – could also assist in achieving the transition to a more abundant local civil society, by recognising time spent in service to the community as a contribution to the fund.

The changes envisaged here, a new welfare model built on virtue and reciprocity, a greater role for local people alongside professionals, a recognition that public services belong properly to local civil society rather than the central state – all require a far greater degree of local social responsibility than England enjoys at the moment. The systems for this exist already, in the vestiges of old methods of community self-government and in more recent innovations. We have parish, town and district councils. We have a vast network of charities and faith groups, trades unions and cooperatives, community organisations of all kinds, including large ones that run hospitals and schools.

New models of local power, including the means for communities to take over public assets or to decide the local planning policy, have been created in recent years. These systems are stronger in some respects than in others, but overall they are far weaker than they should be. Indeed, they are entirely peripheral to the main distribution of power, which makes England the most centralised state of its size in the world.

Given the degree of central control over local government it is perhaps little wonder that councils hoard what power they have and that political cliques and cabals dominate local government to the exclusion of most ordinary people. Despite the vestiges of local self-government, local residents have next to no direct involvement in the management of local life, whether through the formal structures of the local state or through consultations and processes designed to engage the public, or even through the wider institutions, the boards and trusts and committees that respectable local worthies of all classes once sat on as a sign of their duty and status, but which now exercise only petty or ceremonial powers.

This, then, is my last recommendation for the new social covenant. The restoration of the Order as it should exist in our communal life depends above all on the transfer of power from the state to local places. We should insist as the price of this devolution that councils open up decision-making to communities themselves. And the necessary corollary, to ensure that councils are properly representative of and attentive to their communities and that local people give proper attention to the management of neighbourhood life, is paradoxically illiberal: 'council service' should be compulsory.

Just as you already expect to do jury service, every adult should expect to spend a year of their lives as a part-time councillor, whether at parish, town or district level. You would be trained and recompensed appropriately, and chosen through a process of sifting and balance to ensure real representation, and to deny the sharp-elbowed, the monomaniacal, the reactionary and the transgressive too much power. But participation in the social covenant, in the institutions of your place, is not something to opt in or out of. This is your neighbourhood: take responsibility for it, and make it the place you want it to be.

Afterword

IDEAS OF ENGLAND

This book has focused on what Burke called the 'sources of the commonwealth' – the household and the community, the family and the parish – and on the deeper springs of our common life, our ideas about what it is to be human. But what of the commonwealth itself, the larger community that is held together not only through human relationships and some common ideas, but also by law and by the mysterious thing called statehood? What of the nation?

Like the family and the community, the nation is an essential element of the Order we need to restore and renew. Just as the *oikos* and the *par-oikos* represent both efficient units – the right size for independent agency and self-support – and more sentimental objects of love and loyalty, so nations are both effective and affective. They are or should be nimble, operationally independent and equipped with the wherewithal to defend and advantage their members. And they inspire intense devotion, carrying the history of their people and representing a core part of an individual's identity.

This dual understanding of the nation explains the decision of a majority of the British people to vote to leave the EU. Brexit represented both a practical recognition that the modern world demands agile, independent actors rather than cumbersome superstates, and more profoundly an expression of identity, of attachment to this land, its people and its history. Brexit was not a rejection of our European identity and heritage. The 'enemy' for Brexiteers was and is the anti-identity of globalism, the doctrine of international allegiance that has infected not just the EU but progressive elites across the world, and in the UK especially. London, indeed, was as much the object of resistance for Leave voters as Brussels.

The slogan 'global Britain' adopted by some Brexiteers observes this truth in the breach: it was an attempt to obscure or mitigate the anti-globalist impulse behind Brexit. Of course, a legitimate objection to the EU was the protectionist bloc it created, inhibiting our trade and our immigration flows with the rest of the world. But this was not the real objection of most of the people who voted to leave. They wanted to take back control from political elites who not only diminished the nation state but also hollowed out the personal associations, the families and communities that give life its security and meaning.

Brexit authorised the great changes that are needed for the nation state. We need larger armed forces to defend ourselves and our allies; real not theoretical control of our borders; greater resilience in the critical industries; and a leaner, more capable and more strategic central state. And we need the central state to focus on these things – defence, resilience, strategy – not on the delivery of personal services to individuals and families, or the management of the institutions of local neighbourhoods.

The role of government in respect of the personal and the social is to set the framework, creating the conditions in which individuals, families and communities can best govern themselves. As a society we should instruct the state to guarantee that no one will go without, but insist in general that people have the capability and the obligation to meet their own and their neighbours' needs before they look to the government.

If we think of a nation as more than a community of sole traders bound together only by the rules that regulate their dealings – if we think of a nation as something meaningful and valuable in itself – we must ask what it is for. What do we do together, and what do we want to achieve?

We want to achieve the good life. This is meaningful, though imprecise. One cannot define it exactly, yet one recognises the concept and we can name some of its aspects. The good life for the United Kingdom is found in a society

that is broadly equal, both in starting points and in outcomes, but mostly in conditions – where although there is
some natural disparity in wealth and status everyone can be
said to be part of the same community, sharing common
interests, and where everyone has a fair shot at a good home,
a decent job and a stable family.

In a good society there is justice: good is rewarded and
bad is punished. Local life is safe, likewise the life of the
mind, and all diversity of religion and worldview acknowledges the primary authority of the historic culture of these
islands. We tread lightly on the Earth, and for all our right
of dominion we settle in nature as fellow creatures, not alien
overlords.

The good life is the pursuit not of wealth, but of prosperity, properly understood as well-being or flourishing,
which encompasses both material and social, psychological
or spiritual richness. It is found in local relationships, communities of interest and the real freedom that only comes
with belonging.

In England – to speak of just one part of the UK, the
part I belong to – we yearn for all this and we recognise it in
potential, though we do not always see it around us. Indeed,
this vision of the good life is informed and enriched by the
examples of other societies; there is little to boast of in many
aspects of modern England, and much to learn from others.

But there is a certain idea of England, or a set of ideas,
that other nations perhaps recognise quicker than us, and

admire. One idea is the heroic England, which has blazed the trail of freedom at home – the birthplace of the rule of law, mass democracy, equal rights – and exported these things abroad, if sometimes selectively and self-servingly. Another idea is the gentle England, where art and science are safe and honoured, where difference is protected and even celebrated, where there is a special affection for the romantic, the dogged and the loser.

There is the England of dissent and progress, the narrative of our history as the long, hard-won – still to be fully won – victory of the liberal light over the darkness of oppression and inequality. England carries the hope, strong and deep, of a just society, and the conviction that we are, through many tribulations, marching towards this goal and will reach it sometime in this age.

And there is the rival idea, the England of conservation, whose history tells of the protection and transmission through successive challenges of some precious things: the habits of good sense, fortitude, humility and humour, and most of all, the habit of liberty. England is, or should be, a comfortable home for those who feel left behind in the modern age, or intellectually unconvinced by the secular New Jerusalem; who hold no hope for a truly just society but think that we can be the best of a bad lot.

I began this book with a list of anxieties of the great threats that beset the world in general and the UK in particular. These ideas of England – heroic, gentle, progressive, conservative – discordant as they seem yet each recognisably *us*, are the starting points for the great project of defence and restoration that is needed. We can have confidence that if we get our house in order, this defence and restoration will occur.

The Order will revive, refitted for modern times, and win the culture war. The Idea will be defeated, at least for now, and the earnest decent citizens who promoted it will be forgiven and easily accommodated in the restored and settled commonwealth. And so we will achieve what politics is for: a happy, because a virtuous people.

ENDNOTES

INTRODUCTION: ON MORGAN'S HILL

1 A. Case and A. Deaton, *Deaths of Despair and the Future of Capitalism* (Princeton University Press, 2020)

2 HM Treasury, *Public spending statistics: July 2022*. This figure excludes pensions which are also classed as 'social protection'

3 'Households below a Minimum Income Standard', Joseph Rowntree Foundation, 2022

4 Paul Kingsnorth, 'What Progress Wants', The Abbey of Misrule substack, 24 May 2022

5 Yoram Hazony, *Conservatism: A Rediscovery* (Forum Press, 2022)

6 Guy Standing, *The Precariat: The New Dangerous Class* (Bloomsbury Academic, 2014)

7 W.R. Smith, *Religion of the Semites: The Fundamental Institutions* (A & C Black, 1889)

8 Edmund Burke, *Reflections on the Revolution in France* (J. Dodsley, 1790)

9 Andrew Rumsey, *Parish: An Anglican Theology of Place* (SCM Press, 2017)

10 John Bowlby, *A Secure Base: Parent–Child Attachment and Healthy Human Development* (Basic Books, 1988)

11 Paul Collier, *The Future of Capitalism* (Allen Lane, 2018)

12 John Milbank, *Theology and Social Theory: Beyond Secular Reason* (Basil Blackwell, 1990)

CHAPTER ONE: THE IDEA AND THE ORDER

1 Patrick Deneen, *Why Liberalism Failed* (Yale University Press, 2018)

2 Edward Skidelsky, 'The return of goodness', *Prospect Magazine*, 27 September 2008

3 Tom Holland, *Dominion: How the Christian Revolution Remade the World* (Basic Books, 2019)

4 The contribution of Marx and Nietzsche (and Darwin) to the dismantling of the old morality is well explained by Carl Trueman in *The Rise and Triumph of the Modern Self: Cultural Amnesia, Expressive Individualism, and the Road to Sexual Revolution* (Crossway, 2020). Paul Fussell's classic *The Great War and Modern Memory* (Oxford University Press, 1975) shows how the war destroyed the last vestiges of confidence in the ideas of progress and order, whether conservative, Marxist or liberal.

5 Yoram Hazony, 'Where did conservatism go?', James Madison Program in American Ideals and Institutions, 21 September 2022

6 Quoted in Colin E. Gunton, *The One, the Three and the Many: God, Creation, and the Culture of Modernity* (Cambridge University Press, 1993)

7 Alasdair MacIntyre, *After Virtue* (University of Notre Dame Press, 1981)

8 T.S. Eliot, *The Rock* (Faber & Faber, 1934)

9 A.W. Brian Simpson, *Human Rights and the End of Empire* (Oxford University Press, 2001)

10 Jonathan Sumption, 'Law and the Decline of Politics', Reith Lecture 3, 2019

11 *Ibid.*

12 See the judgements in *R v. Secretary of State for Transport, ex parte Factortame* (1990), *R v. Secretary of State for the Home Department, ex parte Simms* (1999), and *Thoburn v. Sunderland City Council* (2002)

13 Judgement in *Ghaidan v. Godin-Mendoza* (2004)

14 Baroness Hale, 'Is the Supreme Court supreme? Nottingham Human Rights Lecture', 2011. A recent ruling by the Supreme Court of the United Kingdom has rejected this view, and confined British courts to an application of the Convention that reflects that of Strasbourg. The pendulum swings to and fro.

15 Roger Scruton, 'The state can't set you free', *The Spectator*, 16 October 2004

16 Bob Hepple, *Equality: The New Legal Framework* (Hart Publishing, 2011)

17 Equalities and Human Rights Commission website, 'Public Sector Equality Duty'

18 Kemi Badenoch MP, Hansard, 26 October 2022

19 Judgement in *Maya Forstater v. CGD Europe* (2019). The judgement was overturned on appeal

20 On 6 December 2022, Isabel Vaughan-Spruce was arrested for violating a 'Public Space Protection Order' around an abortion facility in Birmingham, when it was closed. The case was subsequently dropped.

21 Paul Yowell, 'The Future of Equality: Why it is time to review the Equality Act 2010', Policy Exchange, 2021

CHAPTER TWO: ON SEX AND DEATH

1 Jonathan Haidt, *The Righteous Mind: Why Good People are Divided by Politics and Religion* (Penguin, 2013)

2 David Goodhart, *The Road to Somewhere: The Populist Revolt and the Future of Politics* (Hurst Publishers, 2017)

3 Sigmund Freud, *Civilization and its Discontents* (Hogarth Press, 1930)

4 Trueman, *The Rise and Triumph of the Modern Self* (Crossway, 2020)

5 'Mainstream pornography... coalesce[s] around a homogenous script involving violence and female degradation.' 'The public health harms of pornography', The National Center on Sexual Exploitation, February 2018

6 Gunton, *The One, the Three and the Many* (Cambridge University Press, 1993)

7 Simone de Beauvoir, *The Second Sex* (Knopf, 1949)

8 Philip Rieff, *My Life among the Deathworks: Illustrations of the Aesthetics of Authority*, 2006

9 'Surveys indicate a decline in sex among young adults in Britain', *British Medical Journal*, 7 May 2019

10 Herbert Marcuse, *Eros and Civilization: A Philosophical Inquiry into Freud* (Beacon Press, 1955)

11 'UK natural population set to start to decline by 2025', *Financial Times*, 12 January 2022

CHAPTER THREE: OIKISM

1 David Brooks, 'The Nuclear Family Was a Mistake', *The Atlantic*, 15 March 2020
2 'In parallel with the neutering of women's economic contribution, the post-industrial division of domestic labour also saw the rise of a whole branch of psychiatric medicine devoted to managing the pathological effects that division had on women's mental health.' Mary Harrington, 'Why tradwives aren't trad enough', *UnHerd*, 30 January 2020
3 Germaine Greer wrote: 'Women's liberation, if it abolishes the patriarchal family, will abolish a necessary substructure of the authoritarian state... so let's get on with it.' *The Female Eunuch* (MacGibbon & Kee, 1970)
4 Miriam Cates MP, Hansard, 11 March 2021
5 Brooks, 'The Nuclear Family Was a Mistake', *The Atlantic*, 15 March 2020

CHAPTER FOUR: A NEW SOCIAL COVENANT

1 'David Attenborough – Humans are plague on Earth', *Daily Telegraph*, 22 January 2013
2 Henry Dimbleby, *The National Food Strategy*, 2020
3 *Ibid.*
4 Iain McGilchrist, *The Master and His Emissary: The Divided Brain and the Making of the Western World* (Yale University Press, 2009)
5 Dan Wang, '2021 letter', danwang.co
6 Colin Mayer, *Prosperity: Better Business Makes the Greater Good* (Oxford University Press, 2018)
7 Edmund Burke, 'Letter to a Member of the National Assembly', 1791
8 Chris Renwick, *Bread for All: The Origins of the Welfare State* (Allen Lane, 2017)

9 The Ways to Wellness social prescribing scheme in the North East of England achieved a reduction of 35 per cent in hospital costs over two years for the patients who took part. See 'Ways to Wellness' case study at the Government Outcomes Lab, University of Oxford.